Thorn In My Rose Bush

A must-read for About to Marry,
Just Married and with some years of Marriage

Prof. A.P. Sharma
Seema Gupta

UNICORN BOOKS

Publishers
UNICORN BOOKS, New Delhi-110002
E-mail: unicornbooks@vsnl.com
Website: www.unicornbooks.in • www.kidscorner.in

Distributors
Pustak Mahal, Delhi
J-3/16, Daryaganj, New Delhi-110002
☎ 23276539, 23272783, 23272784 • *Fax:* 011-23260518
E-mail: info@pustakmahal.com • *Website:* www.pustakmahal.com

London Office
5, Roddell Court, Bath Road, Slough SL3 OQJ, England
E-mail: pustakmahaluk@pustakmahal.com

Sales Centre
10-B, Netaji Subhash Marg, Daryaganj, New Delhi-110002
☎ 23268292, 23268293, 23279900 • *Fax:* 011-23280567
E-mail: rapidexdelhi@indiatimes.com

Branch Offices
Bangalore: ☎ 22234025
E-mail: pmblr@sancharnet.in • pustak@sancharnet.in
Mumbai: ☎ 22010941
E-mail: rapidex@bom5.vsnl.net.in
Patna: ☎ 3294193 • *Telefax:* 0612-2302719
E-mail: rapidexptn@rediffmail.com
Hyderabad: *Telefax:* 040-24737290
E-mail: pustakmahalhyd@yahoo.co.in

ISBN 978-81-7806-128-3

Edition : 2007

Printed at : Param Offsetters, Okhla, New Delhi-110020

Introduction

Most human beings are alike throughout the world as far as their husband-wife relationship is concerned. They easily become jealous of each other, fight on small and petty matters, cajole when required and love intimately when they are emotionally and physically in harmony. At times, they also indulge in a short-lived hatred which perhaps crops up on account of unrealistic reasons and misunderstandings. But if the thread of love is strong, it never breaks even if their lives may experience many ups and downs.

All in all, marriage is a great experience in itself. There are ups and downs, there are joys and sorrows and there are tears and peals of laughter which give marriage its spice and flavour. I am sure, all of you married ones will vouch for it, while all you newly married ones listening intently to each and every word I say, will give that meaningful smile to each other, and all of you yet to be married will look towards your future with a bright shimmering shade a head.

In fact, marriage is an alien territory for both men and women. It is slightly more alien to a woman for she leaves her father's home and faces new situations in her husband's home. Husband's home is certainly totally new to her, as she has to accommodate and live with so many relatives of her husband. In spite of the fact that a married Indian woman has to get used to living with so many relatives in her new home after marriage, she, like any other woman in the world, also wants a healthy man, who is loving and extremely caring for her. She wants a man who can make decisions and whom she can depend upon and feel secure. She wants a man who can take care of his family's interests and always act rightly. Perhaps she would not like a man who is just popular and unable to take action when required. She may also not like simply a masculine kind of man who is authoritarian, rough and is merely a controlling kind of person. She often looks in him a man who is caring, who does not share his intimacy with any other woman, and who is trustworthy. Above all, she always prefers a man who does not dawdle when encountered with difficult situations.

At times problems crop up in marriage. It is perhaps the most trying time for both husband and wife. When these problems appear, it is often easier to blame each other than to take responsibilities. It is during these times that one needs to understand that trying times are opportunities for a couple's personal growth. What exactly a man and a woman require to learn in order to grow and strengthen their relationship is an important issue for both of them. That is the main theme of this book. It tells how a man and a woman should jointly face and fight the challenges of life, and how they should react to the various situations in order to keep their relationship strong and smooth. When there is a spell of bad weather in their lives, none of them requires separate shelters. On the contrary, they both need to stay under one umbrella and help each other to ward off the storms that threaten their personal happiness.

In this book, through different men and women, their personal problems are being narrated to enlighten the married couples and tell how men and women react unwisely when they are encountered with difficult situations. Although their prejudices seem to be natural and their reactions true, a thoughtful disposition and an unprejudiced mind would be able to seek better solutions to their so-called problems that often threaten their relationship at times.

—A.P. Sharma

Preface

People marry with a rosy portrait of married life in their mind. The roses they exchange during courtship seem to last forever. The fragrance never seems to fade. They are fascinated with this eternal bliss of love. Considering themselves to be the blessed ones, they take the plunge. The fragrance keeps following them for some time and then suddenly their world turns topsy turvy. The thorns from the rose bush start pricking them.

This was not they had bargained for!!!

This sudden jolt makes them wonder if that was it! Some, who lose patience, end up going back to their single status missing out on all the fun that the coming days could offer.

Those who dare to endure the thorns and wait for spring patiently, so that roses could bloom again, get true happiness once they understand the real meaning of marriage.

Whenever there is a problem in any relationship, it is easier to blame the other person than to take the responsibility. However, it is important for a person to realise that relationship is a mirror, and these challenges are opportunities for strengthening that relationship.

There may be times when you are left wondering if you are the only one facing such tough challenges. But it is not so. Each one of us is riding in the same boat. The only difference lies in our perception of each situation. What you perceive as a threat to your marriage may seem to be a minor hurdle for another couple.

Our book *'Thorn in My Rose Bush'* brings you two versions of marital relationships.

The first part *'Make your married life meaningful'* looks at the marital problems through the eyes of an elderly couple settled in foreign lands. Far from their own country, they are still as Indian in their thinking as any of us living in India. Being a mature and experienced couple, many people come to them for advice and go back well satisfied. The focussed views of the elderly couple, their convictions and their easy camaraderie form the essence of the book. Their advice is well accepted by all the couples who come to them seeking their valued opinion.

The second part of the book *'Not in a long time'* presents a more concise view of marital relationship between a couple who is living in India in the nuclear family structure. The problems posed by modern living standards and their own perceptions threaten their married life. Their marriage seems to be heading towards disaster when the couple gets a breather in the form of a trip away from their routine life. How the elders in the family play an important role in bringing the couple together can only be understood after reading these craftily written pages, which are full of wisdom for youth in today's modern setup of Indian society.

I hope this book will give you an insight on the delicate relationships shared by the partners in marriage. In case you have any suggestions or seek counsel, you may contact me without any hesitation.

Seema Gupta

(s_guptaa@hotmail.com)

Contents

Part - I

Part - II

Part - I

Make Your *Married Life* Meaningful

Prof. A.P. Sharma

Chapter 1

I hate being controlled

Chains do not hold a marriage together. It is threads, hundreds of tiny threads that sew people together through the years

Prabhakar and Bala hailed from Kerala. Prabhakar worked in a road construction company at Delhi as a senior engineer for more than thirty years before coming to Africa. He knew three languages, including Hindi, and could write and speak them fluently. This was one couple who was liked and respected equally by the Indian as well as Pakistani community. Many families visited them, especially in the evening, when both Bala and Prabhakar would sit in their verandah overlooking their small garden.

One evening, an Indian family visited them. They were Kumar and Preeti who had come to the town around two years back. Kumar was a civil engineer working on a building project owned by the State government. Prabhakar and Bala greeted them warmly. When Bala asked them if they would care for some tea, Kumar immediately consented to her offer as he was coming straight from office. While tea was being served, Prabhakar made the guests feel comfortable. But soon after the tea session was over, Preeti moved her chair closer to Bala. Bala could feel that Preeti had something on her mind.

While Prabhakar and Kumar talked about their office and projects, the conversation between the two ladies was personal. Preeti told Bala that she had some problems relating to her husband's behaviour. Most Indian women, when they talk about their husbands, don't confide in anyone else other than their own closest relatives. Mr. and Mrs. Sundaram, being senior in age, were considered as an elderly figure for the Indians living there. So Preeti thought of confiding in Bala.

Preeti felt that her husband was often dominating and liked to control her each and every movement. "Even if I go to the local market, he would tell me what time I should go, with whom I should go and when I should return home," she told Bala in a desperate tone. After a short pause she continued amid sobs, "I hate being controlled by any one."

> If you are sure about something that you consider right, you must clearly express that your opinion implies care and love for the family. It can easily dispel the feelings that you are becoming bossy

Kumar and Prabhakar had stopped their conversation by now, and were listening to the two women. So far Kumar did not say a word but as Preeti started crying, he interrupted and told Bala that what she was telling was not quite true. "I need to check her as she does not know whose company she should keep and with whom she should go to the market," said Kumar, in an angry voice.

Preeti, who had by now partly recovered from her doleful mood, continued accusing her husband persistently. "How do you know that the company I keep is not worthwhile? Do you think Mrs. Rastogi is not a good person? It is she with whom I often go to the market. What is wrong with her? She seems to me quite a friendly and receptive person."

Kumar had considerably recovered from the earlier shock given by his wife. Preeti had also stopped crying after narrating her problems to Bala. After a short pause Kumar explained to her very politely. He said that he had come to that town almost a year before she had arrived and he knew more about most of the Indians living in that town. Without mentioning much about Mrs. Rastogi, who was working in a small company nearly five kilometres away from that town, he continued, "Before one starts keeping someone's company, one ought to know a little more about that person. Mrs. Rastogi is not a bad person, but she possesses a bigmouth and is capable of talking anything about anyone. It is because of this reason that I don't want you to keep her company."

So far Bala had listened to both of them calmly. She did not say a word, to let them vent their anger. When both of them looked towards her for her opinion, she said solemnly, "I reckon Kumar is right to say that we should choose our company carefully. Once when my husband was stationed at Delhi, one of his colleagues' wives started visiting us frequently. My husband did not like her visiting me that often. He asked me to stop her from coming to our house. I did not like him checking me and telling me what company I should keep. Whenever he objected to the company of that lady, I resisted and accused him of being bossy. But soon I discovered that she had started spreading confusing information about me, which resulted in skirmishes between both of us and among some of my husband's colleagues. She possessed a bigmouth and invented stories that were never true."

After a short pause she continued, "By the time I discovered the truth, it was too late. Some of my husband's colleagues had already misunderstood us and turned into enemies." Bala stopped for a while and continued again, "I reckon Preeti, you must not feel as if you are being controlled by Kumar if he gives you some sane advice." Looking towards Kumar she said, "I feel Preeti will listen to your advice more carefully if you talk to her in a friendly way. Besides, you can make her accept your opinion easily if you provide some convincing arguments rather than forcing your opinion on her."

Then Bala went on to narrate certain other incidents that happened in her family when their two sons were very young. If Prabhakar would advise her to keep them away from the company of some of his neighbours' children, she would not listen to him. "I would not listen to my husband as I thought that he was being too dominating. Until I myself discovered that the neighbourhood children were unruly, I did not take his advice seriously. It is always good to make the person agree by providing some convincing arguments. Or let that person discover that what she/he is being told is right."

Then Bala said in a solemn voice, "A family always requires a balance of confidence and goodwill between a husband and wife. If they lack it at any time, several unrealistic problems may crop up between them, disturbing the peace and progress of the family. It is, therefore, better to confide in and listen carefully to the advice given by each other. It is one of the best ways to develop confidence and help the entire family grow with a firm and progressive pace."

She continued addressing both, "If you insist on something, telling what is right and what must not be done, it is imperative that your opinion should imply the good of the family whom you care a lot and love more than anything else. It will certainly solve your problems and dispel the feeling that you are being controlled."

Liberty is the only thing you cannot have unless you are willing to give it to others

❑❑

Chapter 2

Setting the limits

Offer choices as opposed to issuing ultimatums

When Indians live in foreign lands, they love to celebrate certain national functions together and create opportunities to meet each other regularly. It has become more customary after the country attained independence. Out of a couple of national festivals, the Republic Day is often celebrated in its true patriotic spirit. Most Indian families love to gather at an appointed time and at a selected place. They happily celebrate the occasion, participate in the activities sponsored by the organisers of the festival and greet each other with open arms.

It was one of the Republic Days when most Indian families had gathered to witness the flag hoisting ceremony. Besides the many Indian families who had come to take part in the national festival, the Indian ambassador had come to hoist the flag. Mr. and Mrs. Sundaram were formally invited by the organisers and were given due honour as their seats were placed next to the ambassador's seat on the dais.

After the flag hoisting ceremony was over and the Indian ambassador had left, the entire place was open for the visitors and the Indians. Children and women attired in colourful dresses were adding to the charm of the occasion. It was quite a big place where several stalls of food, jewellery and ready-made clothes were put up. Girls between 12-15 years of age participated in several cultural programmes including Indian dances. There were a few toys' stalls too for the smaller children.

Prakash and Ritu, both doctors, working in the government hospital had also come to attend the Republic Day function along with their two small sons aged five and seven named Ravi and Devan. Both Prakash and Ritu being well known to the Sundarams, approached them once the flag hoisting ceremony was over. After the usual greetings were exchanged they requested the Sundarams to visit them one evening, and to have dinner with them. The Sundarams agreed instantly and promised to visit them on the next Sunday.

> Keep in mind that change takes place with time. It is easier to set good value patterns in the beginning of a married life, but it is never too late. What you require is to set norms within reasonable limits and ensure to stick to them

At the appointed hour the Sundarams reached Prakash's house. Before the dinner, all the four sat in their small garden and enjoyed soft drinks for almost half an hour. During that time Ritu excused herself and went to the kitchen to take care of the dinner. It was then that Prakash had a chance to discuss various issues concerning his family with Prabhakar.

Prakash told Prabhakar that it was difficult for him to stop the children and Ritu from making purchases when they went to the market. He narrated that on the Republic Day, the children went wild buying all sorts of toys. Ritu never tried to stop them or made any efforts to distract them. Prakash narrated, "Besides, when Ritu goes to the market, she, too, acts in a wild manner and buys anything, whether needed for the family or not. It not only involves a lot of expenditure but also makes my budget tight. I really don't know how to stop them from extravagance." When Prakash was busy narrating his problem to Prabhakar, Bala too went to the kitchen to assist Ritu, who was giving final touches to the dinner.

Listening to Prakash, Prabhakar said, "Your problem is not extraordinary. It often happens with the children and women if they are not bridled from the beginning. If you want Ritu to act wisely, you should set the limits and tell her frankly that you won't accept her spending beyond a particular limit."

Prakash interrupted at this point and said that he had been trying in this direction in the past, "But Ritu never stops spending money in buying things of little use to the family."

Prabhakar smiled and reflected wisely, "Prakash, remember that change takes place with time. It is easier to set a good pattern at the beginning when you both are committed but it is never too late. Help each other in changing the situations and wait to attain the desired goal."

Then Prabhakar gave an example to throw more light on Prakash and Ritu's problem. He said, "Suppose you are out with your family and your son, Devan, wants you to buy something. You have already bought him a few things and you say you will get it for him next time. But Devan wants it now and starts throwing everything he finds nearby. Would you permit him to act that way?"

Prakash replied instantly, "No. I would tell him if he continues behaving in that way, he would not get it next time either."

"Yes, you are right," said Prabhakar. "He will stop immediately as he knows you will do what you have said. It is a bit too late to set limits for your own family. But once you do set the limits, you must insist on abiding by them."

"Prakash, dinner is ready." That was Ritu calling them for dinner.

"Thank you sir, for your valued suggestions. I'll try to work on them." Prakash thanked Prabhakar profusely as they moved inside for dinner.

We struggle with the
complexities and avoid the simplicities

❑❑

Chapter 3

Accepting full responsibility

Be polite but never let any one ignore your needs and take advantage of you

Arvind was another Indian who frequently consulted Prabhakar in times of distress.

On a previous occasion, when Arvind left them, Prabhakar did not mince words. He told Arvind frankly that he should not accept anyone's bad behaviour if he wants the other to change. Arvind looked quite settled after listening to Prabhakar. Before leaving the Sundarams, he promised to see them again as he wanted more advice from Prabhakar.

When Arvind came again a few days later, he was received with the same affection and politeness. Bala asked him whether all was well at home. Arvind replied quite respectfully, "Yes, all is fine except Neelu's unusual conduct. At times I feel worried on account of her conduct."

Prabhakar was not happy to hear it. As soon as Arvind was comfortable Prabhakar said, "When you are used to seeing things in a certain way, it is hard to look at them differently. Let me explain it to you." Narrating an example Prabhakar said, "Immediately after our marriage I used to blame Bala for her conduct and the way things were between us. I would blame her upbringing. That means I was indirectly blaming her parents. At times I blamed her friends too for influencing her conduct."

At this juncture Arvind instantly interfered, "I too do that, for I feel it is on account of Neelu's upbringing that she behaves like that."

Prabhakar continued, "But Arvind, is it possible to change Neelu's upbringing now? Could you really change what her friends have been telling her? You actually need to learn to look at things from a different perspective. You need to look at your own actions. If you could see clearly how you were handling things, you would certainly change yourself first."

Prabhakar paused for a while and continued, "Being the head of the family I had to take full responsibility for making things better and changing my wife's conduct, as at times it did not suit our family."

Prabhakar continued, "Taking full responsibility also meant that I would not give in to her on something that I knew was not right, and then turn around and blame Bala when things went wrong. In fact, it has been happening for hundreds of years when man blames woman for his own mistakes. In the beginning of a married life a man is so fond of his wife that even though he knows that she is wrong, he accepts it."

> When you submit to your partner, you often do it to seek his/her approval. That means you are fully responsible for the partner's bad conduct. If you don't really seek his/her approval, you must learn to say "No" firmly, politely and with certainty

Listening to the basic truth explained by Prabhakar, Arvind at once commented, "Yes, you are right. So many times I have given in to Neelu for the sake of keeping peace in the house, thinking that she will appreciate me for it. Later on when it turns out badly, I blame her."

Prabhakar laughed in a friendly manner and said that he was not blaming him for what was happening in his house. "I am simply telling you that you need to understand clearly what you really want. The moment you understand that, you are responsible for changing the situation. In fact, neither your friends nor your parents want to listen to your complaints. How would you react when you hear a man complaining about his wife's conduct? You would certainly think that the man is becoming unmanly."

Arvind understood the hidden meaning behind Prabhakar's advice. Desperately he uttered, "What should I do now?"

Prabhakar replied solemnly, "Better ask yourself, Why did you submit to your wife? Do you really want her approval? If not, you must learn to say 'No' firmly, politely but confidently. It will not only help Neelu to understand what you actually want, but will also cultivate respect for you in her mind. It has helped Bala and me to improve our family's environment. Although she did not change overnight, it did work in due course of time."

It was quite late by the time Arvind left them to go home.

Trust and be trustworthy.
Keep your promises

❑❑

Chapter 4

You need to show leadership

There is nothing nobler or admirable than when two people who see eye to eye keep house as man and wife, confounding their enemies and delighting their friends

It so happened that Arvind, out of curiosity and ardent desire to understand his personal problems better, visited Prabhakar once again within a couple of days. In fact, he went to his office this time. That particular day, Prabhakar was extremely busy until afternoon, so he asked him to come back after 3.p.m. Arvind reached Prabhakar's office at the appointed hour, who offered him tea and went to the office library to have an informal chat with him.

Arvind, who desperately wanted to talk, told Prabhakar, "My wife is often criticising me without any serious reason. She says that I am not doing enough, and often waste time in doing several things that are not important for her or any of us. At times I don't have any desire even to go home. I really don't know what is waiting for me there."

Prabhakar, listening to Arvind's story, smiled as he was reminded of similar kinds of events that had happened years ago at home when he and Bala were newly married. He said, "This sounds so familiar. Let me narrate my experience with Bala, who is really a wonderful person. Years back I was not sure how to handle my problems at home. So I would permit Bala to run the whole show. One day she abruptly said that I was not doing enough. Suddenly I realised what she meant by that. In fact, I was not showing any leadership. I was hardly making any decisions at all. I was leaving everything to her. She wasn't happy at this. She did not want someone controlling her things, but she also did not want someone who left it to her to run the show. Keeping that in mind I learnt certain good lessons."

Prabhakar continued, "The first lesson I learnt about making Bala happy was to understand clearly what I wanted and how I wanted to handle things." He continued, "Even if she always showed her disagreement with me, she wanted me to be her full partner in all matters. She wanted to look up to me. She wanted me to be strong and not someone who simply wanted to please her. If I was right and made decisions, she would surely respect me."

> The irony is that if you are trying to please your wife, you are not really pleasing her at all. If you show her you know what you want, you will get more respect from her

Arvind was listening to Prabhakar attentively. In the meantime there was a telephone call for Prabhakar. After attending his call, Prabhakar resumed talking. He said, "It has been going on for thousands of years."

Arvind laughed at that and said, "Italian dictator Mussolini ruled Italy during the Second World War, but his daughter used to say that her mother was the real dictator of the family."

Prabhakar nodded and continued, "Yes, it is the same old story throughout. Even my father, who was considered a strong man, would often dislike opposing my mother's decisions. But it does not mean that one should get scared to take decisions or for the sake of pleasing the other, should skip taking the right decisions. It will not be fruitful at all to please the other person. If you try to do so, your partner will surely comment some day that you are not doing enough. It will hurt you more. It is, therefore, imperative to take responsibilities and make decisions rather than try to please the other."

Agreement is the power to life

❑❑

Chapter 5

She is turning the kids against me

The greatest thing a father can do for his children is to love their mother

The Sundarams went home during December, after taking one month's leave. They had to attend their nephew's marriage in India. When they reached India they met many relatives including their two sons who by then had almost settled there. Kapil, the older one, was working as a scientist in one of the leading computer companies at Hyderabad. The other son named Narendra had completed Masters in Chemistry. He was trying to get a job in a leading university in Kerala. Both Prabhakar and Bala were extremely happy to see their children.

The marriage was over just one week before the Sundarams were supposed to leave for Africa. At that time one of Prabhakar's younger brothers, Deepak, who lived in a nearby town, came to visit them. Both Bala and Prabhakar welcomed Deepak warmly. When Deepak was settled in his chair, he started conversing with Prabhakar confidentially. He said, "Brother, I am in trouble. I need your help and advice."

Prabhakar anxiously inquired, "What is it? What has happened?

Deepak said, "It is about my wife and my two children, Satish and Neena. You know both of them are now grown-up and have completed their education. My son is a teacher and my daughter has appeared in the final examination of Masters in

History. I am trying to fix her marriage soon. Both my kids are nice, obedient and affectionate. I have spent a lot of money and time in bringing them up but they don't listen to my advice. Often they are against what I tell them. I reckon my wife has been turning them against me. At times I feel very desperate when the children don't listen to me. I really feel very frustrated."

Prabhakar inquired, "Why is it that your wife has been setting the children against you? It means she too has not been listening to you."

> Giving in to your spouse's undue desires would not only aggravate the situation, it will also ruin your relationship with your spouse and children. Children will listen to you more and abide by you if you and your spouse both work together and take decisions hand in hand

Deepak accepted that his wife, Leena, does not listen to him either. "At times she is so wild in her conduct that I get scared. Then I have to yield to her desire. Last night she insisted that I buy a costly ornament for her. I am really not in a position to spend so much money to buy any ornaments for her or anyone else. When I refused, she started screaming and shouting so loudly that the neighbours could easily hear her. Fearing that she would unnecessarily make a show, I had to promise her to buy the ornament she has been pestering me for long." Deepak continued after a pause, "If I make any mistakes, she does not let me forget it. I keep giving in and then I become ready to give up. I give up for I think it is easier just to go along."

Prabhakar smiled after listening to his brother's woeful story. He reflected, "Deepak, what you have said is not new. I also used to think it would be easier just to go along with Bala whenever she made some similar shows in the beginning of our marriage. I thought it would bring peace. But I was wrong. Instead, I lost her respect when I gave in to her undue demands."

After a short pause, Prabhakar continued, "Peace does not come from always giving in. Besides, the children also need to see that their parents respect and support each other. I remember a case of an Indian friend who is now working in the US. He married an American lady who always opposed him whenever he tried to advise the children to improve their unruly conduct. The result was that the kids, instead of improving, gradually deteriorated in their behaviour. Their grades in school went down and they often indulged in quarrels with their classmates. Since the wife always supported the children against her husband, the children gradually turned against him."

As soon as Prabhakar stopped to take a long breath, Deepak inquired, "What happened after that?"

Prabhakar looked at Deepak and continued, "The friend was quite intelligent. He did not lose courage and finally repaired the situation. He held a couple of intimate sessions with his American wife and explained clearly to her that her interference, while he instructs the children to improve their conduct, will lead to disaster finally. Anyhow, he was able to explain to her that she was wrong and she must at once stop interfering when he instructed the children. It would give the children an impression that both the parents were alienated in taking decisions against or for them. And believe me, it worked. It may not work immediately but it will surely do. When both the parents react with the children jointly, it makes the children easily understand their own position in the house. It works very well to change them for the better."

When Prabhakar stopped, Deepak heaved a loud sigh and said, "I tried to explain to her what you are telling me, but she did not agree with me and continued to interfere."

Listening to Deepak, Prabhakar told him, "She did not improve because you told her all that half-heartedly. If you had explained to her firmly, you would not have required telling her all that repeatedly. It makes a lot of difference."

Deepak left his brother's house with renewed confidence and promised to come back to see them before they left for Africa.

It so happened that Deepak came to see the Sundarams a day before they were leaving India. This time his wife Leena was also with him. Deepak seemed to be relaxed and Leena also looked calm. Deepak thanked his brother and sister-in-law for being kind to him. He also expressed his thanks to them for some very productive advice. He said, "Brother, I have no words to express my heartfelt thanks for your timely and invaluable advice. It seems to have worked."

A father's responsibility is not to make his child's decisions, but to let the child watch him make his

❑❑

Chapter 6

Be a model father for your children

Children will not always listen to you, but they will always imitate you. Fathers who punish children for doing wrong, when they haven't taught then how to do right, are themselves wrong

It was the morning of the day, when the Sundarams were getting ready to leave India for Africa. There was a chaotic scene in their house. Several relatives poured in one after the other to bid them farewell and wish them 'happy journey.' The Sundarams were delighted and welcomed them with open arms. Tea, fresh fruits and breakfast was served to all. Then the couple started making preparations to catch the evening flight. Most guests left by noon except one named Anil, who was Prabhakar's first cousin and whom Prabhakar loved very much. Bala asked Anil and his wife Kamala to take some rest in their bedroom that was not yet totally winded up. But Anil did not like to waste time in taking any rest. He wanted to discuss one of his pressing problems with his senior cousin, Prabhakar. As soon as Anil got a chance to talk to Bala, he requested her to ask Prabhakar to spare half an hour for him for he needed to discuss his very personal problem. In fact, it was Kamala who was more eager than her husband to discuss their problem.

Soon Bala got a chance to talk to her husband about Anil's request, and Prabhakar agreed to talk to him around 3 p.m., until then, to let them all rest.

At 3 p.m. Prabhakar went to converse with his cousin and his wife. Anil and Kamala were already waiting for him. After he was seated, he asked Anil what it was he wanted to discuss. After a short pause Anil said, "I do everything for the children and my wife, but they have a feeling that I could do more. At times I also think that way, and desire earnestly to do more than what I have been doing. What more should I do to make them happy?"

Prabhakar listened to Anil carefully and said, "You are not the first person to think that way. You will have grief and misery if you think that money and property are enough to make you a true father of the family. In fact, my father was the role model for me. He did everything to make me happy. Yet there were so many things that he could not provide me. But I never blamed him for that. For me he was a model father. More than providing material things it was his leadership role that inspired me in my life. At times he disciplined me too but such occasions were few. Some women always complain to their husbands that they are reluctant to discipline their children. But disciplining children is not only teaching. It is much more than that. It is the father's leadership role that is more important for the children. It is managing, training, correcting and also occasional punishment, which is far more important for them rather than fulfilling material needs."

> More than disciplining the children, a father needs to provide them leadership and training and correct them whenever they require to be corrected. To have an ideal influence on his children and to cultivate good relationship with his wife, he must be first of all a father

After a short break Prabhakar continued, "If a father has to have an ideal influence on his children and wants to have a good relationship with his wife, he must be first a father, which simply means to be a leader of and a model for his children."

Anil interrupted at this point and said, "I have tried my best on these lines but I feel that I have not reached a point where my family may look up to me as a leader."

Resuming his conversation Prabhakar said, "If a father tries to prove himself only as a good-natured father, he deprives his children of a strong model to pattern themselves after. He also deprives his daughter of a good male model pattern on which she could build her future relationship with a male, particularly with her future husband."

Anil and his wife interrupted at this point and asked, "What should be done then?"

Prabhakar replied, "You need to guide your children. You need to teach them what is right and wrong. You need to educate them to deal with the challenges of life. You must help them to grow up. That is what fathers did thousands of years ago and it is what is required even today."

The conversation lasted for more than an hour. It was time for them to leave as the Sundarams needed more time to make final preparations to go back to Africa. Anil and his wife left them after saying their good byes.

The father who does not teach his son his duties
is equally guilty as the son who neglects them

❑❑

Chapter 7

Listening to wife is also important

Success in marriage does not come merely through finding the right mate, but through being the right mate

The Sundarams started getting ready to drive to the nearest domestic airport to take a flight that would take them to Delhi from where they would board the international flight for Africa. They reached the domestic airport two hours earlier as Prabhakar did not want to miss that Particular flight. Before they reached the airport Anil and his wife were already there to see them off. The Sundarams were more than happy to see them as they had plenty of time to board the plane.

When all the four were comfortably seated, Prabhakar told Anil, "It is good that you are here. During our previous conversation I forgot to tell you something very important."

Anil chuckled and inquired informally, "What is that?"

Prabhakar Sundaram, after a moment's pause, said, "It is also important to listen to your wife and both of you should make decisions together."

Anil interrupted, "Do you think it is very important?"

Prabhakar continued, "Yes, women have always been respected in our country from ancient times and so is their opinion. A group of teachers in Babylonia wrote that in some matters a man should make decisions, and in some, the woman should decide. A woman's advice is valuable but it does not mean that your wife should decide every matter. If you always automatically follow her advice without using your own judgement, she may lead you astray."

Anil once again interrupted, "Is it so?"

Parbhakar said, "Your sister-in-law Bala is a smart person. I value and appreciate her opinion, but I don't always do whatever she says. At the same time I learnt that if I want to be a strong person, I had to be open and listen to my wife. But I must use my judgement even though I listen to my wife's advice and value her opinion. Sometimes I need to be flexible too and compromise. Other times, I had to be firm."

> You must be careful not to hurt your wife's feelings. You should also listen to her. It is also imperative that you should not be led by her advice without using your judgement, for following her totally may lead you astray

After a moment's pause Prabhakar continued, "It is not only important to listen to your wife, but it is equally important that you don't hurt your wife's feelings by being curt and disrespectful to her."

Prabhakar had hardly finished his last words that his flight was announced. They picked up their handbags and boarding cards and said good bye to Anil and his wife Kamala. As they proceeded towards the gate to board the plane, both Anil and his wife stood in a corner of the airport to see them off. Anil stood there for a few moments for he was still thinking about what his older cousin had advised.

A happy marriage is no accident. It is a result of a deliberate effort by the husband and wife to build a lasting relationship through little acts of care and concern

Chapter 8

You can make things work

Think before you react. A humorous, understanding, or neutral reaction can defuse a potential problem, while a defensive, angry, or irritable reaction can incite an argument

The Sundarams flew from Delhi to Africa via Rome after three hours of landing at Delhi by the domestic flight. When they reached the African town, they were received by their several friends and colleagues. It was customary that the Indians settled there would offer dinner for several days to the family that came back from long leave. The main purpose of that kind of hospitality was to help the newcomers to settle down. At one of these dinner meetings the Sundarams met a couple of Indian families who had recently arrived.

Every evening when the dinner party was thrown by a host, the entire environment was full of merriment and festivity. Once again Prabhakar happened to see Arvind and his wife during one of these parties. They exchanged meaningful smiles when they met. Arvind and Neelu paid them due respects in the traditional Indian manner.

Prabhakar asked Arvind, "How did you do during the time we were in India?"

Arvind replied, "Pretty good. I tried hard to follow your advice. I feel things are improving a lot."

Prabhakar was happy to hear it. He then invited Arvind and his wife for dinner at their residence two days later, for he liked talking to them. "In fact, I don't have anything special in my mind but I simply desire to see you both as I have not seen you for more than a month," said Prabhakar.

Both Arvind and his wife were happy to receive the invitation and agreed to see them sometime the next week. When the guests started leaving the hosts' place, the Sundarams also left for their home.

It was the next Tuesday when Arvind and Neelu went to see the Sundarams. After initial greetings Prabhakar began, "When I saw you after a long time, I suddenly remembered something which I thought was important for you to know as it would help you improve the quality of your life and make you live happily."

Listening to Prabhakar, Arvind and Neelu felt delighted. Arvind, desirous to know something new, hastily asked, "What is that important thought?"

> If you wish to make things work for you, you ought to transcend to be worthy and strong within so that your wife gets merged within you and unifies with you to be as a one whole

Prabhakar commented, "If you are strong enough your wife will always like to go with you and will stop flying in the opposite direction as often you feel. Instead, she will be your helper when taking decisions about family matters."

Arvind, not clearly understanding Prabhakar's message, inquired anxiously, "What do you mean by it? I did not follow you completely."

Prabhakar explained, "I mean to say that if you were strong within, your wife will always co-operate with you and work like a helper instead of opposing you." After a moment's pause, Prabhakar continued, "A wise man living in France in the eleventh century wrote, 'If you are worthy, the woman will be a helper. If you are not worthy, she will be against you.' In other words, it is up to the man to make things work for him."

Both Arvind and Neelu were looking at Prabhakar with admiration. In the meantime Bala announced that the dinner was ready. Prabhakar concluded, "Man and woman are two opposites. If a man is worthy, they may unite into one whole. But if he is not commendable she will be against him because they are made of opposite stuff. Therefore, if you wish that your wife should listen to you and think that you are worthy, you ought to be strong to handle the problems. That is the way to make things work for you."

Bala once again announced that the dinner was already laid on the table. Prabhakar stopped talking and all went to the dining table to take dinner.

Marriage – that relation between man and woman in which the independence is equal, the dependence is mutual, and the obligation is reciprocal

❑❑

Chapter 9

A woman wants her man to possess backbone

The great secret of successful marriage is to treat all disasters as incidents and none of the incidents as disasters

A good number of days passed when no one came to see the Sundarams after they had completed the dinner rounds to their friends. It was Sunday afternoon when they were just relaxing in their garden. All of a sudden a car stopped in front of their house. Hari Prasad and his wife Dwarka came out it. Before entering their house, Hari Prasad asked Prabhakar if they were bothering them by their sudden arrival.

The Sundarams were really polite and good-natured people.

Prabhakar instantly replied, "Not at all. You are most welcome to your friend's house."

When both were seated Prabhakar asked them, "How are you both? It has been many days that we have not seen you. It is good that you came today."

Prabhakar's manner of conversation was so polite and homely that both felt at home instantly although it was their second meeting. Hari Prasad replied with gratitude, "You are really very kind. We both appreciate you for your kindness and hospitality. Besides, your talk is full of wisdom and sane advice, which actually impelled us to visit you again."

Both Bala and Prabhakar Sundaram were happy to hear that. Prabhakar said, "Well, you are my countrymen and therefore, it is my duty to tell you what I feel is right. I don't think I said something extraordinary that day when you met me first but if it helped you, I am delighted."

Listening to Prabhakar, Hari Prasad stated, "Sir, I liked your advice how a woman should be judicious when she opens her mouth to talk, but today I have a few other queries to make. When I try to take charge, Dwarka criticises me. She often wants to control me. If I give in, she does not feel happy. Instead she resents. What should I do under these circumstances?"

Prabhakar laughed heartily after listening to Hari Prasad. Bala also joined him. Hari Prasad and his wife felt as if Hari said something which was funny. He queried instantly, "Do you think I said something funny?"

> If you wish your wife should admire you, you must grow stronger. A woman often tests her man to find out if he is strong enough and possesses a backbone with which he can stand straight to protect her when required

"No not at all. We did not laugh because you said something funny, but we laughed at the way you said it. You showed as if your problem is immense and cannot be solved," said Prabhakar.

Hari Prasad, smiling at Prabhakar's remark said, "I felt that I have a big problem so I came to take your advice. Hope you will think about it and tell me what to do under such circumstances when she does not like my controlling a situation, and when I give in, she starts resenting."

Listening to Hari Prasad, his wife felt as if her husband was criticising her. She at once said, "I don't think you are right. I hardly try to control you even though you try to be bossy at times."

Hari Prasad replied, "I am not saying that you really try to control me. But you do try to criticise me if I take charge of a situation. When I just submit to you, you resent that too."

As soon as Hari Prasad finished talking, his wife started getting amused at his way of narrating the facts. The Sundarams once again started laughing but this time their laughter did not last long.

Then after a moment's pause, Prabhakar commented, "Perhaps she behaves like that because she likes to test you whether you really have a backbone. If you don't have a backbone she will resent you. If you don't have a backbone, it means you are not strong enough to protect her when she requires protection."

"Remember Hari, everything that happens to us in life is a trial. It is, in fact, a test that we should see as an opportunity to grow. Every new situation provides us a new challenge that pushes us to find strength we did not know that we had. The bigger the test, the more opportunity it provides us to grow if we fight it out."

Both Hari Prasad and his wife looked at Prabhakar Sundaram admiringly. They seemed to be all praise for him. The ideas he was reflecting upon were matchless and highly valuable. Prabhakar continued, "Hari, listen. If you grow strong enough and become more confident, your wife would neither criticise you nor would she resent you." It was such a pleasant and realistic conversation that both Hari and his wife felt extremely happy and convinced.

As soon as Prabhakar stopped talking, Bala brought tea and some refreshment for them. Both the guests enjoyed fresh tea and sweets and left for their home after some time.

Balance is the key to life

❑❑

Chapter 10

A woman admires a man who is manly

The grand essentials of happiness are: something to do, something to love, and something to hope for

During weekdays Prabhakar Sundaram was often busy with his work and his wife Bala was also busy in fulfilling the family needs. She needed to go to the market a couple of times to buy grocery and other stuff required during the week. As she did not know driving, she had to take help from one of her neighbours, Rukmini, who would take her in her car any time she needed and also gave her good company when Prabhakar had to go out of town on business. Rukmini did not live very far from Bala. It was a three-four minute walk to her house from Bala's residence. Therefore, whenever she required help, she would fix her program with her, come back home and wait for Rukmini to pick her up for the market at the appointed time.

Rukmini's husband, Raghwan, was a manager in an oil drilling company. They looked quite affluent by the manner of their living. Raghwan had come around five years ago. His salary was quite high and they possessed all the modern amenities a rich family could have. Although Raghwan had a lucrative and respectable job, he did not show off about it any time. Both Prabhakar and Raghwan were highly paid Indians, but both of them were gentlemen who possessed great human qualities, worthy of admiration by their own community as well as African people.

Prabhakar, out of the two, was well known among Indians as he would often join functions, social gatherings and parties thrown by his own people. Raghwan was comparatively busy with his job to spare much time to attend parties or social functions. Even on the function of the Republic Day of India, he had to be offshore to assist other workers.

One of the working days when Bala went to the local market to pick up some grocery, Arvind and Neelu met her when she was about to board Rukmini's car. Arvind requested both of them to come to their place which was not very far away from the local market. But Bala expressed her inability to visit them at that time, as she had to prepare lunch for her husband that afternoon. Prabhakar did not often come home for lunch but that day he was somewhat free in his office. He had promised his wife to be home for lunch. Therefore, she was in a hurry. But both Rukmini and Bala promised them a visit the following day.

Next day both Rukmini and Bala accompanied by Prabhakar reached Arvind's house. It was almost 6 p.m. Neelu and Arvind were waiting eagerly for them. Prabhakar asked Arvind how his work was going. Arvind smiled and said politely, "Sir, everything is fine at home and at work." Then after a moment's pause, he queried, "How about you?"

Being manly means having confidence and self-reliance. It means having high moral standards, being self-disciplined and possessing strength of conviction. It also means being honest and having courage to fight problems that encounter one's family time to time

Prabhakar responded, "All seems to be good at my place too, except that some workers occasionally create some problems. But everything is under control."

Since Raghwan was often absent from parties and social gatherings, Arvind asked Rukmini whether he was fine. Rukmini replied, "Oh yes, he is good. He is out of the town for a week on offshore drilling. He will be back on the coming Monday."

The truth was that many Indians had hardly seen Raghwan though they had heard about him a lot. Arvind was really very eager to see him. He requested Rukmini to bring him to their place whenever it was convenient to them. Rukmini promised that she would. Then Arvind, directing his question towards Prabhakar, inquired, "What are those qualities that command respect for a man from a woman? I reckon it is a macho man who is more liked and respected by most women. What do you think about it?"

Listening to Arvind's query Prabhakar thought for a while and reflected, "Arvind, in fact it is not the macho man who is liked by a woman, but it a manly man who is desired by her."

Arvind chuckled at Prabhakar's remarks and asked, "What do you mean by 'a manly man'?"

Prabhakar explained, "Do you have any idea of the two Pandavas – Bheema and Arjuna who belonged to the Mahabharata days. Bheema was a macho man but more than he it was Arjuna who was liked by women as he was a manly man."

"Could you kindly throw more light on the qualities of a man known as manly?" asked Arvind.

Prabhakar thought for a while and narrated, "To be manly is to possess the noble qualities of a man who is mature in character. It means to have the admirable traits of being respected. A manly man is he who possesses courage and has an independent disposition. The Oxford Dictionary also defines a manly person in that way."

At this point Arvind showed his disagreement with Prabhakar and said, "I have never heard that a manly man possesses noble qualities. What are those noble qualities then?"

Prabhakar's countenance became solemn at this point. He said firmly, "A manly man means to have a matured character, to have high moral qualities, to possess self-discipline and decisiveness, and to have strength of convictions. In fact, if you want to be manly you have to be worthy of being honoured, which means to possess honesty and reliability." After a short pause Prabhakar continued, “To possess courage is to be able to deal with difficult situations, and not backing out on account of fear of pain or fear of any sort of danger. To be independent is to be confident and self-reliant as well.”

Prabhakar’s conversation reached a point where Arvind did not have any more questions to ask. Instead, he was smiling after getting convinced by Prabhakar’s explanations about the definition of a manly man. In place of asking questions, Arvind tried to supplement Prabhakar’s definition of a manly man by adding the following few words to it.

He said, “It is because a man doesn’t possess a manly disposition and lacks the strength of conviction, his woman may not respect him. I reckon, what you have said just now is absolutely right. A man has to be decisive, possess courage and strength of conviction so that his wife should respect him and listen to him. For it is such a man who will not only command respect from his woman, he will also be honoured by others and will be worthy to fight against odd situations that encounter a family, time to time.”

Prabhakar Sundaram was all pleased to listen to Arvind’s supportive reflections. He said, “Well said Arvind. Keep it up.” At this point all got up and took leave from Arvind as it was quite late in the evening.

If you don’t ask for it,
don’t get upset if you don’t get it

❑❑

Chapter 11

The one who gives, loves truly

A successful marriage requires falling in love many times, always with the same person

Whenever Prabhakar was out of town, Bala would receive many calls from friends if she needed any help. In fact, in a few years the Sundarams had earned a great respect from their own countrymen as well as from the others. As a result, Bala never felt that she was all alone. There was hardly any evening when one or two families would not come to visit her. If people are good-natured and kind to others, they mostly receive respect and love from them.

It was during one of the days when Prabhakar was out of the town, that Bala requested Rukmini to take her to the market. When they finished buying groceries and other important items and were about to leave for home, they were spotted by Arvind and Neelu. They requested Bala and Rukmini to come to a nearby restaurant to have some refreshments. Both of them refused to go with them as they had finished shopping and required to go home as they had to do a lot of work at home. But as Arvind and Neelu went on insisting, they conceded to their request and agreed to go with them for half an hour.

When they reached the restaurant, Arvind ordered tea and light refreshments for all and started talking casually. He inquired, "When will Mr. Sundaram come back home from his tour?"

Bala answered, "He will be back on Sunday. Do you need to see him?" she asked him.

Arvind said, "No, not really, but it is always a great pleasure to see him."

Bala responded, "Oh, thank you Arvind. You are such a nice person that my husband often remembers you too."

Delighted, Arvind replied, "I feel so good myself after talking to him." Then he directed his attention towards Rukmini and inquired about Mr. Raghwan. She replied that he was fine and added that when he would get time from work, they both would like to visit them.

Arvind was even more delighted to learn that they were planning to visit them and thanked her for it. In the meantime all of them finished tea. As they were about to leave, Bala told Arvind in a solemn voice, "It is always good to give people, for in return they also give you something. You have very kindly offered us tea and refreshments. In return you have won our love and respect." Then after a moment's pause she commented, "The more you give, the more your love grows. When Prabhakar and I started our married life, he used to bring several gifts for me. But more than the gifts, I cared for his sincerity and attitude with which he cared for me. In return my heart would come out for him. I always used to think how I should return my love for him. It led me to understand that I should cqually take care of him and never let him feel that he was left alone."

> Problems begin when married couple become receivers only and turn back from being givers. The truth is that love and giving go hand in hand

Arvind interrupted and commented, "But do all wives and children whose parents give them a lot, equally love them in return? Sometimes the kids who receive a lot seem to resent their parents the most."

"Arvind, love flows in the direction of giving. In fact, love and giving go hand in hand.. We might think loving leads to taking because we often see people believing in receiving more when they are in love with someone. The truth is that it is the other way around. The one who gives, loves truly," said Bala.

Arvind felt delighted to listen to Bala. He commented, "I am beginning to understand what you are talking. But still I have something on my mind that I wish to tell you."

Bala said, "Please go ahead."

Arvind inquired, "Why does love not seem to last?"

Bala seemed to be amused at Arvind's query. She replied politely, "After a while the initial feelings of love start losing their grip. It is a delicate change that most lovers don't notice clearly. At the beginning there is love and giving. But gradually they go back to being takers and each one starts making demands on the other. When demands ensue, love disappears. I, therefore, strongly believe that if a couple desire to continue loving each other, they ought to give each other strong love."

It was such an excellent talk by Bala Sundaram that not only Arvind and Neelu felt indebted to her for enlightening them but Rukmini also felt thankful to her. Rukmini immediately expressed her feelings and commented, "Sister, I never knew that you possessed so much wisdom. I feel grateful to you for giving me such a great precept that if you love, you must learn to give. So far I too used to think that my husband is not caring for us as he is always busy with his work. When I look at it now, I really feel bad for my inadequate understanding. In fact, whatever time he devotes in the company, he gets its returns. Literally, all those returns are for us only. He has been constantly giving us but we don't understand it." She then thanked Bala profusely for her nice talk. She thanked Arvind also for offering them refreshments. After a while they all departed to their homes happily.

Giving your family your time
shows respect for them

Chapter 12

Goals give you purpose to live

Support each other to achieve personal goals. If you help each other grow as individuals, you'll grow as a couple

As time passed many families started feeling attached to the Sundarams as their manner of responding towards them, whenever they were in any kind of need, was full of warmth and affection. Prabhakar never turned his back to anyone if he came for any advice or help, irrespective of any community or country he belonged to.

It was one of those evenings when Bala was aimlessly chatting with her husband in their garden that Ram and Savita came to see them. Both of them were doctors and had come to the town a couple of months back. They had met the Sundarams once during the Deepawali festival when most Indians organised and celebrated the festival at one place. As soon as Ram stopped the car in front of the Sundarams' house, they were received with warmth by Prabhakar and directed to their garden where they were seated a minute ago. After the exchange of a few casual questions, Prabhakar asked Ram and Savita if they had something important to talk.

Ram responded leisurely, "Right now we don't have anything on our minds. We just came to see you. We saw you once during the Deepawali festival but after that we never got any chance to visit you. Though it is a bit late to visit anyone, but without thinking of your inconvenience we just stopped by."

Prabhakar responded affectionately, "It is good that you came to see us. Yes, I remember we met last year at Deepawali. As I often go out of the town on account of my work, we are not able to visit people as often as we both desire. You are most welcome to our place."

Both Ram and Savita were delighted to listen to Prabhakar. In the meantime Bala told them that she would be back soon and went to the kitchen to check if she could offer dinner to the guests. She came back to the garden in about two minutes and asked Ram and Savita if they would kindly like to have some light dinner with them.

> Contemplate seriously with your mate about what you want to achieve in life and plan to follow those goals in spite of difficulties. Your goals will give you the direction and purpose that will keep both of you together when you have hard times

Looking at Bala, Savita told her that it was not their intention to visit them so late to have dinner with them. But Prabhakar went on to ask Ram to stay although, he said, it would be just an informal and light dinner.

Considering that the Sundarams were very earnest in their request, Ram consented finally. When her husband agreed to stay for the dinner, Savita offered Bala to help her in the kitchen. Both the ladies worked very fast to heat up the leftovers. They also cooked a fresh dish and a few *chapatis* so that all would enjoy the dinner. The table was set by Savita and both Ram and Prabhakar were told that the dinner was ready and placed on the table.

They ate the dinner in half an hour and went back to the garden to chat. While they were talking Ram told Prabhakar, "I am planning to start a farm house in my town in India and also to send my only child to a public school in Dehradun."

Prabhakar waited for a minute if Ram had anything else to say. When Ram did not comment further, he responded, "It's a good idea to have a farm house at home for it may generate good income in future. It is also an excellent idea to send your son to the public school at Dehradun. It is a very reputed school in India. Parents, who can afford and who wish to give good education to their children, plan to send their children to the Doon School."

"It is good to have goals in your life, for goals give us purpose to live our lives. Without goals our life will run like a wild animal that has no direction or place to go. If we have goals, we direct our energies to run our lives in that direction and achieve them for the benefit of our children and family," continued Prabhakar.

Ram said, "I have not thought yet that far. I am simply planning to do so, but if it leads us towards a good end, I will really feel great."

Prabhakar commented, "Ram, you must know what you want and have a plan to get there. So, better think it over many times carefully and execute your plan after you finalise it. When we had started our married life, we repeatedly talked about our goals. We talked about how we wanted to raise our children and how we were going to earn and spend money. It is better to discuss goals many times with your wife."

"It is a good idea. So far we both have talked about our plans very casually, but it seems a good idea to discuss the goals seriously and plan carefully to execute them," said Ram.

Prabhakar continued, "Having goals will give you a purpose in life. It will help you keep going in hard times. Ram, believe it or not, we too had hard times in our lives. But it is because we had decided to attain our goals that we continued going, in spite of hard times."

After a moment's pause, he said, "I really learned to plan what we wanted to achieve and tried hard to execute it. Our goals helped guide us when we had to make decisions. Without any goals, we could have been driven to any direction in our lives."

Ram and Savita felt that their visit to the Sundarams was quite enlightening. When it was almost eleven in the night, they departed after thanking them for a good dinner and fruitful conversation. Before they left they promised to see them again whenever it would be convenient to the Sundarams.

If you share a dream, help make it a
reality even if it seems impractical.
No dream is impossible or impractical.
Impractical does not mean unimportant

❑❑

Chapter 13

Don't live beyond your means

Most marriages are not made in heaven, they come in kits— and you have to put them together yourself

Prabhakar Sundaram took his wife to a nearby resort for two days as Friday was declared a local holiday by the State government. Fortunately Rukmini and Raghwan were also with them to enjoy that small break. As Raghwan was too busy with his off-shore duties, Rukmini never had any opportunity to go for an outing since they came to that town. Since both the families were quite close to each other, they were looking forward to utilise that small break fruitfully. Both the ladies made a few preparations in advance by cooking some dishes so that they would not waste time cooking at the resort. There was a beautiful lake by the resort where small boats were available for the tourists. Both Rukmini and Bala loved boating.

As soon as they reached the resort, they checked into their separate rooms. In fact, Raghwan had already phoned to the hotel manager to keep two rooms reserved for them. It was nice and cozy inside the rooms as they were fitted with all the modern amenities. First, the ladies took shower and both the men got ready in their swimming suits to swim in the lake. By the time they reached the lake the sun had started to set. All helped in taking out the foodstuff from Raghwan's car. Bala and Rukmini gradually started preparing for the evening tea for there was still time for dinner.

Both Raghwan and Prabhakar were good swimmers. They spent almost half an hour swimming in the lake, until then, the ladies kept themselves busy with talks relating to their kith and kin. When both the men came out of the lake, tea and light refreshments were ready for them. The four of them enjoyed it by the side of the lake and indulged in aimless talks for they had plenty of time on their hands. After tea they decided to go for boating. When they returned from boating, the ladies served dinner which all the four enjoyed for almost an hour amid gossips and light talks by the lake side. After dinner they came back to the resort. Before retiring to bed they planned for the next day and decided to visit another tourist place which was hardly fifty kilometres away from that place.

> Be careful in spending money to buy things which you earnestly require. Don't buy things which you cannot afford. Never buy things to compete with others. Financial stress can create problems at home and ruin your family peace

The two couples got up early next morning and were ready to leave for the scenic spot. They had carried some working lunch on the way, so they planned to rest until 5 p.m. and decided to go to the lake in the evening. When they reached the lake in the evening, the male folk did not like to go for swimming. Instead, they decided to go for boating and to spend time in gossips. When they came back after boating, the ladies served the tea. As they were sipping tea, all the four started looking at the setting sun. In a few minutes the sun went down leaving behind its fading light. A few clouds had already gathered in the sky. Both the ladies and the men sat there in silence. The beauty of Nature made them quiet. They did not feel like talking to one another for a long time. Obviously their attention was captivated by the beauty of the setting sun. The sky looked superb and it greatly fascinated them because Mother Nature was changing colours each moment.

It was Prabhakar who first broke the silence. He said, "Raghwan, how are things at home?"

Raghwan, taken aback by Prabhakar's abrupt question, looked at him for a moment and answered casually, "Well, all seems well, except for a few things."

"What happened? Do you have any problems?" inquired Prabhakar Sundaram.

Listening to Prabhakar, Raghwan said, "Yes, there are some problems at home. In fact, I built a house in my home town in India. Being a novice in the field of house-construction, I planned for a big house which cost me a lot. It made me take a huge loan from the bank. The monthly instalments towards the repayment of the loan are so heavy that at times I get stressed. The bank's repayment policy is very stern. If I missed any of the instalments, the bank could impose great penalty on me. It would be disastrous for my family and me. Unfortunately, we both have fought many times over this issue. She goes on accusing me for my wrong planning and I go on explaining the reasons why I made such a big mansion in my home town."

Prabhakar Sundaram listened to Raghwan attentively and thought about it for a couple of minutes. Then he replied in a rather low voice. "Dear friend, all people make mistakes. But the best thing would be to think how to amend it. Our forefathers have always warned us to avoid problems that lead to arguments at home. They advised us: 'Be careful with family finances, because quarrels are likely to erupt at home due to financial stress.' Financial problems can aggravate problems in a marriage and shatter the family's peace to any extent. I am really grateful to my wife who has always been very careful in spending money. She does not buy things that we cannot afford. She has always been advising me how and when to spend money. We never try to live beyond our means. It has saved me from indulging in unnecessary financial burdens at home and abroad as well. For example, when I decided to buy a new car, she always thought about our immediate requirements and family status. It led me to take a correct decision when I bought a new car over here."

"Yes, you are right, Prabhakar. Rukmini did advise me to build a moderate house in India, but I did not listen to her and finally got entangled in financial problems. Is there any way to get redeemed from that sort of problem?"

"Yes, there are ways to release your financial stress. But before that I would like to tell you a real story of one of my neighbours who was always buying furniture, new cars and all kinds of things they really did not need. At times I envied him. He was always buying. But soon I discovered that he was ultimately not happy. Eventually he could not make the payments for the instalments of the bank loans. Consequently, his car and furniture were taken back by the bank he took loan from."

Then after a moment's pause he continued, "Your problem can be solved by applying to the State government for a reasonable amount of loan that may help you to pay the total loan you took from the bank at home. The State government of this town provides to its workers a considerable amount of loan on easy instalments and at a very low interest. Try it."

Raghwan had never thought about it. He felt elated with the idea given by his friend and thanked him for that. After that Raghwan felt much relieved from his personal problem that had been bothering him for a long time. They enjoyed at the resort the next day and left for home happily on the day after.

Watch a sunrise at least once a year

❑❑

Chapter 14

The final discourse

There is no relationship without compromises. When two individuals with different personalities, backgrounds, and experiences make a life together, compromise is a great exercise in respect

Prabhakar and Bala Sundaram had come to that African town around six years back. It was time for Prabhakar to renew his contract with his company. If Prabhakar signed for the third time, he would be required to stay on for another three years. Considering his wife's weak health and commitments at home, he was thinking seriously to go back home, but he was not able to decide. As days passed on and the time to sign a new contract was quite near, he thought to discuss with his wife whether he should sign another contract for three years. One fine morning he said, "Bala, I am in a fix and unable to decide whether I should sign another contract."

Bala was the kind of person who clearly understood her responsibilities at home too. Therefore after a moment's pause she replied, "If you take my sincere advice, I would say that now we need to go back home. Not only that, our eldest son's marriage is overdue, your parents are also very old now. We need to look after them. Better let us go back."

Although Prabhakar had almost decided to go back home, Bala's remarks made him take a final decision. When the old friends learnt about Prabhakar's decision they were surprised and upset. They started visiting them after learning that they would be leaving the town soon. Prabhakar, after consulting his wife, decided to throw a dinner party to all the friends who had been close to them. He, therefore, invited most Indians and a couple of fellow native workers' families three days before leaving for India.

Most Indian families who were in the town that day came to the dinner party. They had mixed feelings of joy and dismay. Joy, because Prabhakar and his wife left an indelible impression of their goodness and hard work with which they kept their country's image high. They saw in Prabhakar and Bala a combination of intelligence and wisdom. Whenever they needed their help and advice, both were ready to provide. But after they were gone there was none to whom they would come to consult when encountered with problems. So they were sad too.

Almost all the ladies who were invited with their families reached the Sundarams' place in the afternoon to help Bala. It was quite an occasion of festivity and dolefulness. Occasionally, the ladies would start crying and spend their emotions before Bala for she would be gone in a couple of days. Bala also could not hide her emotions that day, and wept like a child in front of the ladies who obviously loved her very much. Thus, amid crying and intermittent laughter, the dinner was prepared by the ladies. Most menfolk gathered around 7 p.m. that day as they wanted to spend more time with the hosts.

When the dinner was over, all the guests gathered around the hosts in their garden. Many of them had brought gifts for the couple. When the gifts were given away to the Sundarams, a few senior persons spoke a few words in honour of the hosts. It was time for Prabhakar to say a few words to his friends too. But for a few moments he was unable to speak as he seemed to be charged with emotions. After controlling his feelings he spoke in a solemn tone.

"Dear friends, I don't have many words to thank you for the kindness and love you have shown to me and my wife during our stay in this town. I never felt that I was out of my country all these years, as most of you were always with us whenever we needed you." He stopped for a minute for his eyes were full of tears. Regarding his composure he continued, "I remember the many evenings we enjoyed in the company of Raghwan, Arvind, Hari Prasad, Ram, Kumar and others. I also remember how I tried to give you my advice when you came to me to discuss your personal problems. You were kind enough to listen to me and tried hard to handle your problems in line with my opinion."

Then after a short pause he said, "I shall never have any chance to talk to you again so closely about your personal problems in future after today. I am not a priest. Nor do I possess the wisdom of a philosopher. Whatever I have, I have learnt from my personal experiences. So I wish to reflect upon a few things once again before I leave this wonderful town."

After a moment's pause he continued, "If you wish to lead a happy married life, you must never deviate from the family norms and try to listen to your wife too. In return, she ought to abide by you in every matter without criticising you. It is also imperative that a man must act in a manly way and try to control his finances by spending according to his limits that he has already set. A married life is a sacred union between a man and a woman. Therefore its sacredness must be kept in view before bringing disharmony to it. Cultivate confidence between each other by unconditional love and respect for each other. Remember that when you really love someone, you ought to give more rather than desiring to take more. If some of these precepts are kept in mind, you will never fail in life in delivering goods to your family and children."

With these words Prabhakar once again thanked his guests and bade them good bye.

❑❑

Part - II

Not In a Long Time

Seema Gupta

Chapter 1

You are my sweetheart

A happy marriage has in it all the pleasures of friendship, all the enjoyment of sense and reason, and, indeed, all the sweets of love

'Meeta...Meeta...!' Virender called out to his wife.

'Coming...' Meeta came out of the kitchen wiping her hands on her saree. She was busy preparing *paranthas* for breakfast when Virender called out to her. A little flour was smeared on her forehead.

'What's it...?' she demanded as she came near her husband who looked up from his computer. He was smiling at her.

'How beautiful you look with this white *tilak,*' he mused.

'Is this why you called me out of the kitchen? My *parantha* must be burnt by now,' she chided him, though secretly she enjoyed his attention. Giving him a miss, she turned back to the kitchen, when Virender tried to attract her attention.

'Meeta, let Dayaram cook *paranthas,* I called you here to tell you that Ravi is coming tonight. I just now received his e-mail.'

'Really, that's great news.' Meeta's eyes lit up at the news of the arrival of their only son.

'Are Richa and Avi also coming?' she asked.

'No, only Ravi is coming. He is coming here to attend a conference. He will be with us for two weeks,' Virender replied.

'Hmmm... Good.' Meeta barely managed to say this when Virender looked up from the computer and smiled at her, 'I know what you are thinking. He will be here for our marriage anniversary. He remembers it. He mentioned it in the mail.'

'I wish Richa and Avi could also come. Anyway...' Meeta sighed. 'How long are you going to work on your computer? You will be late for office,' Meeta chided her husband.

'Just a few minutes more. Ask Dayaram to bring my breakfast here,' Virender said.

Virender and Meeta were married for thirty-five years now. They had two children – a son Ravi and a daughter Ritika. Ravi was married to Richa and they had a son named Avi. Ravi and Richa lived in Delhi. Ravi owned a garment factory there.

> There are only three basic methods of communication: word, gesture, spirit

Virender and Meeta's daughter Ritika was married to a software engineer Sudeep who was settled in the US. Ritika had a son and a daughter and they were all living in Los Angeles.

Virender was a chartered accountant. He came to Bangalore six years back when he joined this MNC. He liked the place and people here. The work environment was good and he had immense job satisfaction. The only problem was that they missed Delhi and most of all, their son Ravi.

Thought of Ravi brought a lovely smile on his lips when he suddenly noticed his wife standing there, holding the breakfast tray in her hands.

'Look who's smiling quietly. I know you. By now you must have counted the hours and minutes to Ravi's arrival. What time is Ravi's flight?' Meeta teased Virender putting the tray on the table beside the computer.

'Precisely after eleven hours and thirty minutes, right sweetheart.' Virender replied candidly while Meeta blushed and the husband-wife duo burst out laughing.

Friendship, not romance, holds a marriage together

❑❑

Chapter 2

Keep your cool

The secret of having a good marriage is to understand that marriage must be total, it must be permanent, and it must be equal

'Ravi, my son. How are you?' Virender hugged his son as he came out of the airport lobby.

'I'm fine, Dad, how've you been? Where's Ma?' Ravi touched his father's feet and looked around.

'She couldn't come. I had a meeting so I thought I will pick you up straight after office.' Virender led Ravi to the car, which was parked nearby.

'You sit, I'll drive.' Ravi sat on the driver's seat. Virender gave him a loving look and opened the other door.

As the car started moving, Virender noticed that Ravi was unusually quiet. It was not like him to sit quietly.

In order to initiate some conversation, Virender started enquiring about Richa and Avi.

'Why didn't you bring them too? It would've been so much fun. It's been a long time since we got together,' Virender said.

'How can I force anyone to do something out of their choice.' Ravi said bitterly.

'What's wrong Ravi. Is everything all right between you and Richa.' Virender felt alarmed.

'Dad, since Richa picked up this job as fashion designer, she has changed a lot. She was so sweet and demure until she was at home. However, in the last few months since she joined this export house, she has changed completely. She doesn't care for me. She doesn't look after the house; she has no time for Avi. All that she can think of is her work. I also work. Does that mean I forget my family and other things? I asked her to come with me to Bangalore as your anniversary also falls during these days, but she was too busy to take a few days off.'

Ravi was like an uncontrolled burst of dam which seemed to have found a gateway in the sympathetic company of his father.

'You had a fight with her before coming?' asked Virender in a matter of fact manner.

'In fact, I did. How do you know?' Ravi looked at him in surprise.

'It's my thirty-fifth wedding anniversary son. These thirty-five years have taught me a lot.' Virender smiled.

'Richa and my marriage has completed five years and I don't think it's going to make it to six,' Ravi said wryly.

'Come, let's have an ice cream,' Virender said, out of the blue.

It was a game between father and son. Whenever one of them was in a bad mood, the other would offer him ice cream to lift his spirits.

They stepped out of the car and breathed in deeply. The nip in the air felt refreshing.

'Two Cornettos.' Ravi ordered the vendor.

'Nice and cool, isn't it. Tell me son, what's troubling you?' Virender asked Ravi, as they both enjoyed their ice creams.

'Dad, Richa has changed so much. She just does not give me any importance. Like a few days ago, I had to go for a business dinner. I asked Richa in the morning to get my clothes ready for the evening. When I came back from office in the evening, she was feeding Avi. I asked her for my clothes, she showed me my blue shirt, suit and tie lying ready on the bed. But the dress code for the meeting was black so how could I wear the blue suit! When I asked her to iron my black suit, she got into a bad mood. She told me clearly that she had her hands full with Avi, so it would be better if I ironed the black suit myself. Dad, she could have fed Avi ten minutes later. As it is, I was getting late for the meeting. This infuriated me no end. I lashed at her for not looking after my needs well. She retorted back and soon there was unnecessary verbal fight between us which could have been avoided if only she had…'

'… if only you had earlier told her to iron your **black** suit instead of **any** suit,' Virender cut short his son's narrative.

> Mind your P's and Q's. Be polite. Please and Thank you are the magic words. Use them to bring the magic back to your married life

'I forgot Dad, but she could have done it then. It would not have taken her more than ten minutes,' Ravi said sheepishly.

'So could you, my son. Why didn't you? In fact, any one of you could have done if your egos had not come in between.' Virender continued, 'You see Ravi, you should be clear in giving instructions when you want the other person to do something specific for you. This is true in every field of life. In the office, if you do not give clear instructions to your secretary, she might send a wrong letter on a wrong address. Am I right?'

Ravi nodded.

'If you can be so careful in the office then why be so vague in dealing with your wife at home which is the pivot point of your life?' Virender said emphatically.

'Are you trying to say I am in the wrong?' asked Ravi.

'Not at all. Such things happen in married life. You are two individuals with different perceptions and ideas. But remember one thing, to make your marriage work you must not take the other person for granted. I would not justify Richa in not ironing your suit. You were in a hurry, but did you tell her your urgency? Instead of shouting at her, if you had talked to her in calmer tone, I am sure she would have co-operated with you. Son, what is important is keeping your cool and knowing your mind. Several such situations come in married life and pass, if you know how to tackle them.' Virender paid the ice cream vendor and started towards the car.

As they were opening their doors, he smiled at his son and showed him the chocolate ice cream brick he was holding in his hand and said, 'In marriage, one must learn to remain as cool as this ice cream.'

'Hey, we just had one. You bought another one!' Ravi said.

'This is for your mom, silly. She too loves ice cream.' Virender smiled.

'These are the little gestures which help in keeping the tempers cool and relationships hot,' Virender winked at him.

As Ravi started the car, he thought of the loving relationship his parents shared.

Had he ever thought of bringing something for Richa, out of the blue?

NOT IN A LONG TIME.

You know the depth of loving
by the degree of giving

❑❑

Chapter 3

Humour in your fight

To keep your marriage brimming, with love in the loving cup,
Whenever you're wrong, admit it; whenever you're right, shut up

Just as the car reached the portico, Meeta opened the main door and came out to greet them. As Ravi touched her feet, her eyes filled with affection. She was seeing her son after a long gap.

'Have you not been well? You've lost weight,' Meeta asked him as she led them both inside.

Before Ravi could answer her, Virender shook his head.

'You mothers would never learn. You can never say: 'O my child, you look well-fed and looked-after today.' Even if your child is looking like a plump pumpkin, you will call him a thin *kakdi.'* Meeta glared at him while Ravi chuckled. Handing the ice cream carton to Meeta Virender winked at her. 'Here, take this brick and keep it in the fridge and feed it to your son after dinner. Ravi, go to your room and freshen up,' saying so Virender started towards his room.

Suddenly he turned back and said, 'And do not forget to call Richa that you have reached here safely.'

Meeta heard him but kept quiet. She could sense that there was something amiss. But she decided to bide her time. She wanted to speak to her son only after he settled down.

Dinner was a lavish affair. Meeta had cooked everything Ravi liked. Dinner ended amidst loads of fun and laughter.

Once or twice Meeta tried to talk about Richa but Ravi changed the topic.

It was almost 10.30, the threesome was still talking when Virender said, 'I feel like having a cup of coffee. Do you want some Ravi?'

'I don't mind,' Ravi replied.

'Dayaram has gone; I'll go and make it.' Meeta was about to get up when Virender asked her to sit down, 'You gossip with your plump pumpkin. I'll make the coffee.'

Ravi smiled. It felt good. The warm cocoon of his loving family seemed to envelop him whenever he was with his parents. Suddenly his attention was diverted. Meeta was talking to him.

> Most of the time, it's not *when* you are arguing but *what* you are arguing about that creates the problem. Try to see the flip side of the situation and let *humour* take over *angry* emotions

'Why didn't you bring Richa and Avi with you, Ravi?' she asked.

'Ma, she was busy.' He could not muster enough courage to tell his mother that his wife wouldn't listen to him.

Meeta had sensed the sadness in her son's voice. But she was wise enough not to broach such a delicate subject so soon. So they kept talking about other matters, catching up on old times, when Virender entered with the coffee on a tray.

'Here you are.' He handed over a cup each to both of them. Picking up his own cup, as he was about to sit down Meeta asked him, 'Did you put the milk in the fridge?'

'Definitely, my lord,' he replied.

'And closed the lids of the sugar pot and coffee bottle?' she again asked.

'Of course, how can I forget? After that incident, I would never ever forget to do so,' Virender was smiling. 'Now do I have the permission to sit down?'

'What's this about, Dad? What happened?' Ravi asked him.

'I'll tell you later. First of all, you tell me if you have ever made coffee in your house,' Virender asked him in return as he settled down on the couch with his cup of coffee in hand.

As Virender put this query before Ravi, his face hardened. He recalled the day he had made tea for himself and Richa.

> *It was a beautiful day. Being a Sunday, they were both in a relaxed mood. Richa was sleeping. So Ravi decided to make tea for both of them. He went into the kitchen and made two cups of tea. Though the tea came out well, his untrained hands could not keep Richa's spick and span kitchen clean. After drinking tea when Richa went inside the kitchen to place the cups in the sink, she was horrified at the look her kitchen presented before her. Milk was spilled all over the kitchen slab and some of it was spilled on the floor. Grains of sugar were lying on the floor and gas stove where many ants had gathered, trying to carry their evening meal with them. Tea had boiled over on the gas and the burner was drenched in it. Though seething inside, Richa tried to keep her cool and got down to clear up the mess. As she picked up the bottle of sugar to keep it in its place, the lid opened up because it was not tightly closed. The bottle fell down and broke into pieces. All its contents spilled on the floor. Hearing the commotion Ravi came into the kitchen. And what a fight they had afterwards.*
>
> *She - accusing him of being so careless, he - blaming her for picking up the bottle with its lid and breaking the bottle. All in all, the sweet cuppa they had shared a few minutes back had turned into a nightmare.*

Ravi's reverie was broken when his father shook him by the hand and offered a penny for his thoughts. Seeing no point in hiding it, he shared one more thorn pricking in his heart with his parents in the hope that it would ease his burden.

Hearing the whole story, his father started laughing loudly. His mother was giggling too. Ravi could not see any humour in the situation. But before he could say anything his father raised a hand to stop him.

'You know Ravi, I too tried to help your mother many times. Today you may admire my cooking skills, I mean my tea and coffee are not so bad! Right!'

Meeta and Ravi both nodded in agreement.

Virender continued, 'But I remember one incident very clearly. Once we gave a party at home. The maid had not come. After the guests had left, I offered to do the dishes while your mother cleared the table and put both of you to bed. You were small at that time. As I was doing the dishes, I came across a pan that was badly burnt. I was very tired and the pan would not clean. Since your mother was not there, I decided to leave it and do it in the morning. Now you know your mother, in fact, for that matter all women are alike. They do not like their kitchen dirty at any point of time. So I filled the pan with water and hid it in the bottom drawer with other clean pots and pans, leaving the sink looking clean and clear, so that when your mother came into the kitchen she would find everything in order and ....'

'I will take over now.' Meeta cut him short, 'He did not tell me about the pan and I was actually pleased with the look the kitchen presented. But as I tried to take out another pan from the same drawer to boil milk for Ritika, I happened to topple that dirty pan and its water fell all over the place. I understood it was his handiwork, but decided to overlook it because otherwise your father had done a good job of cleaning the kitchen. I knew he was trying to be helpful. Though it took me quite some time, but I quietly cleaned the dirty water from the drawer and cleaned that pan too and then went to bed where your father was snoring blissfully. The next morning I was woken up by the loud noise of pots and pans coming from the direction of the kitchen. When I came into the kitchen, I was shocked to see the drawer sprawled on the floor. All my neatly arranged utensils were scattered on the floor and your dear father was searching frantically inside the drawer for something. What that dirty pan hidden inside the drawer last night could not do was done by this ghastly sight of having my orderly kitchen in shambles. I lost my cool and demanded an explanation from your father.' She turned to face her husband and smiled.

'I too was young then. I also lost my temper. But after hurling a few accusations at each other we both realised the humour in the situation and started laughing. We realised it really wasn't worth a fight but it definitely was worth a good laugh,' Virender said.

'Yes, Ravi, fights are normal in a married life. But if you try to see the humour in fights over silly things, you will fight less and laugh more.' The wise words spoken by his mother set Ravi thinking.

When was the last he laughed with Richa?

NOT IN A LONG TIME.

In the heat of pressure, problems loom larger;
crises seem more severe

❑❑

Chapter 4

The enchanting red roses

When we truly love someone, we allow them their own thoughts, interests and space. We give each other room to breathe

'Cuckoo…cuckoo...!'

The sweet voice of the cuckoo filled the room.

Ravi opened his eyes. The sun was shining brightly. He got out of bed and headed towards the window. The warm sunrays felt good on his face. The calmness and serenity that surrounded this place always exhilarated him. He looked around. How he wished Avi and Richa were here with him, but …

'Ravi, here's your tea.' Meeta came inside his room carrying a cup of tea in her hand.

'Thanks, Ma. Where's Dad?' Ravi asked, sipping the hot tea.

'Today is Sunday, so he's busy with his babies,' Meeta smiled.

'Babies! What babies?' Ravi looked at her in surprise.

'Don't look so alarmed, son. He is in the garden tending to his roses. He got these bushes from an exhibition and they have turned out to be his prized possessions. Now he spends every Sunday morning with them. See, there he is. You can see him tending to those bushes.'

Meeta pointed towards Virender who was busy working in the garden. Ravi placed his empty cup of tea on the table and looked out of the window. He could see the silhouette of his father at a distance in the garden.

'But where are *my* babies Ravi?'

Meeta's question made Ravi turn around.

His mother was watching him intently, 'Yes, my Richa and Avi. Why didn't you bring them with you?'

'Ma, Richa was too busy and...' as Ravi started, Meeta stopped him midway.

'Ravi, don't give me all this crap. I'm your mother. I can sense from a mile when all is not well with you. I can read it in your eyes. Tell me what's wrong,' Meeta patted his hand affectionately.

Now Ravi could not hide things from his mother who was his confidante since his childhood.

'Ma, I recently got a big order from a client who has offices all over India. To co-ordinate things, I had to travel a lot. I had to be away from home for almost twenty days in a month. As you know, Richa has taken up a job recently. Since I have my office on the ground floor of my bungalow, it was not difficult for us to manage home and Avi. All was going smoothly when suddenly this order came up and I had to devote more time in travelling to the various outlets of my client. Initially Richa managed with the maid and took leave whenever I was out of town. But my trips were long and her office could not give her so much leave at a stretch. In the meantime, the maid also left. So we decided to put Avi in crèche. Some time back I finished with my order and now I am back home with the usual work that does not require me to travel. I told Richa to find a good maid and let Avi stay at home with the maid. But she refuses to see reason. She is adamant that Avi should continue going the to crèche so long as she's in the job,' Ravi said.

'Do you mean to say that Avi still goes to the crèche?' Meeta was astonished at the thought of Richa sending her cute little grandson to the crèche.

'Exactly. Richa has become very stubborn, Ma. She does not listen to me at all. Actually this is what sparked the fight before

I came to Bangalore.' Having found a sympathetic ear in his mother, Ravi went on to narrate his tale of woe which was simmering within his chest for the past two days. Meeta waited patiently for him to speak further. She had been biding time since last night for this very moment. She knew Ravi would himself open up before her.

'As my program to come to Bangalore was fixed, I told Richa to take leave for fifteen days. She said that she would try. Then she never told me whether she got the leave or not and I also forgot to ask her. Assuming that we would be going together, I booked the tickets for all three of us. Day before yesterday I told Richa to pack things so that there was no last minute rush. She looked at me in surprise and told me that she and Avi won't be going, as she did not get leave for fifteen days. She said that she and Avi might join us later. This enraged me so much. Why couldn't she tell me earlier when I was booking the tickets and making other arrangements? Moreover, who is she to decide in every matter as to what and how things should be done? She tries to have her way every time. I couldn't control myself and shouted at her for being so careless so as not even bothering to inform me. At this, she shouted back at me in the same tone. Poor Avi got so frightened at our shouting and accusing one another that he stood in one corner listening to our fight which could have been avoided if Richa had listened to me. After that, we did not speak to each other. I got so angry that I did not even say 'bye' to her before coming,' Ravi's eyes had turned misty.

Meeta patted her son on his back trying to console him when suddenly she saw her husband's shadow behind Ravi.

Virender had been listening to their conversation all this while and they hadn't even noticed him.

'So this is what had you so upset yesterday,' Virender said.

'You tell me dad, is it fair on Richa's part to be so dominating. Every time she wants to have her own way. I don't like it at all. After all, I am the man of the house. She should....'

Virender stopped Ravi midway, 'Yes, you are the man of the house and she is the lady of the house. That is where your thinking differs. I heard everything you told your mother. I could even see her sympathising with you when you told her about Avi going to the crèche. But you tell me one thing Ravi, what's wrong in it?

'Why are you so much against it? If Avi continues to spend a few hours in the crèche then why is it bothering you so much? Just because Richa has refused to comply with your orders! But if you think this over with a cool head you will understand that Richa is being more practical. She has no maid. She cannot get so much leave. How will you manage the child on your own?'

'She can arrange for a maid and after that Avi can stay at home under my care,' Ravi offered.

> Make use of the romantic spectacular gifts nature offers you. Find time to share these gifts together

'First of all, it's not easy to get a good and reliable maid to whom you can entrust your small child. Then, you have your own business to look after. You are expanding your business. What is the guarantee that you will not get another such order that requires you to travel? How will Richa manage then? In such a case, she is only left with the option of leaving her job. If that is what you intend to do then why did you give her false promises of co-operating with her when she took up this job? It was on your initiative that she took this job. You wanted her to become a smart working woman like other wives of your friends. Now you are finding fault with her. Do you think it is fair?' Virender spoke to his son in clear words.

'Today Avi has adjusted to the crèche he is going to. If you take him out now, and then circumstances force him to go there again, do you think it is good for a small child to go through so many adjustments at this tender age?'

'But Richa should at least be polite to Ravi. Why didn't she tell him that she did not get leave so she would not be able to accompany him to Bangalore?' Meeta could not see her son being let down by her husband when he needed their support.

'Yeah, I agree, she should have been more communicative, but so could your son, who took her for granted knowing her commitments fully well. Communication gap brings many problems between the couples. Remember Meeta, when these kids were small and I had to go to Hyderabad on an official trip?' Virender looked at Meeta, who nodded at her husband.

'How can I forget those two days. It was a nightmarish experience.'

'When, Dad? I don't remember,' Ravi asked.

'Of course you don't remember because you are not even aware of that incident. You were quite small at that time, but today you are old enough to understand all that happened. There was a marriage in your Nani's family at Pune. We were invited. It was the year-closing time in my company; the audit was going on and there was no way that I could spare time to go to Pune. But your mother was adamant. Although she had the car and driver at her disposal and could have easily gone with you kids and attended the function, she refused to see reason. Initially I felt good that my wife loved me so much that she wouldn't go anywhere without me but as her pestering went on for more than a week, I too lost my cool and told her in clear terms to do whatever she wanted to do but I would not be able to spare time to go with her.

'We had this showdown at night and the next morning I went to my office as usual. When I came back from office in the evening, I found her letter on the table. She was gone with both of you. I felt very bad as she could have called me up in the office and informed me about her programme. Since I was also in a bad mood, I did not call her up at Pune, neither did she call from there to inform me of her safe arrival.

'It so happened that I was asked to accompany the auditors to our company's headquarters at Hyderabad the next morning itself. We left by the noon flight. Until then there was no communication between your mother and me; obviously, I could not inform her about my trip to Hyderabad. Rest is her side of the story. Meeta, do you want to tell your son…?' Virender smiled at Meeta.

Meeta smiled back, 'O Ravi, I was so naïve at that time. After reaching Pune I kept waiting for Virender to call me up. When he did not call me the whole of next day, I swallowed my pride and called up home but there was no reply. I thought he had changed his mind and was coming to Pune. I kept waiting for him another day but there was no sign of your father. I tried to contact him the next day, still no reply. Being a Saturday, his office was closed. There was no other way I could get in touch with him. Now I was really worried.'

'Why didn't you call him on his mobile?' Ravi asked instantaneously.

'There were no mobiles in those days, son. We were at the mercy of the telephone department.' Meeta smiled. 'Then I called up my neighbour who told me that the house was locked and all was quiet. It was too much for me. All sorts of bad thoughts kept haunting me. I could not enjoy the wedding in such a state. So I rushed back home on Monday itself, the day of the wedding. I opened the lock with my key and entered the house. Everything was exactly the same as I had left it. I was about to call Virender's office when I heard someone trying to unlock the door which I had bolted from inside. I rushed to the door and opened it and whom do I find standing there – your dear father, with a bouquet of red roses in one hand and suitcase in the other. Seeing him hale and hearty made me breathe easy and I started crying inconsolably. Slowly he explained to me that he was away to Hyderabad and did not call because he thought I was very angry with him. I was still very angry but all my anger evaporated when he said that he only went to Hyderabad to wind up some urgent work and now he had come here to change and then leave for Pune. He even showed me the flowers, which he intended to carry to Pune for me. There were so many things I wanted to say to him, so many accusations I wanted to hurl at him. I wanted to show him how hurt I felt with his uncaring attitude but his one smile and those lovely flowers melted me. I realised my folly too. I, too, had behaved in a childish manner. If only I had not put that communication barrier between us then I would not have had to bear so much stress for those three-four days,' Meeta concluded.

'...And you could have enjoyed the wedding also which you missed,' quipped Virender.

'Don't you talk about that wedding. My cousin still berates me for going away from her wedding midway. It was all your fault. If you had told me about your trip to Hyderabad, I would not have imagined all those things...'Meeta said.

'Now what were *those things*...may I know.' The twinkle in Virender's eyes made Ravi smile.

Meeta too smiled and looked away.

'Coming back to 'communication barrier', Ravi, I asked you to call Richa and inform her about your safe arrival here. Did you call her last night?' Virender asked his son.

Ravi shook his head, 'Why should I? She also knows that I have come here. She could have called me up.'

'That she did. She called me at midnight when you were fast asleep in your room. She enquired about you. She is definitely more sensible than you. She has made an effort to cross the communication barrier that you had put between the two of you and make a fresh beginning. She said that she had got leave sanctioned for a week,' Virender told his son.

'So she will be here for your anniversary party!' Ravi asked quickly.

'Yes, in fact, she said she will be here before that, so that she could help your mom make arrangements for the party. Today is 10th, she and Avi will be here on 16th and the party is on the 20th, so there is plenty of time.' Virender smiled at Meeta who was listening quietly to their conversation.

'Why so smug, queen bee, here are some flowers for you.' In a dramatic style, Virender handed over one of the two huge red roses to Meeta. 'This one is for not calling you from Hyderabad that day.'

Then he picked up the other one. 'And this one is for giving me this idiot of a son who seems to have acquired all those silly traits of mine.'

Meeta burst out laughing holding both the roses in her hand.

Ravi looked at the flowers. Then he looked at his parents. His mother looked so happy holding the roses given by his father.

When did he last give roses to Richa – on Valentine's day…No….; on their wedding anniversary…Nah..

NOT IN A LONG TIME.

When you and your spouse have a disagreement, regardless of who is wrong, apologise. Say, "I'm sorry I upset you. Would you forgive me?" These are healing, magical words

❑❑

Chapter 5

I love you

A good marriage is one which allows for change and growth in the individuals and in the way they express their love

'Ding dong!'

'Auntie.....! Auntie...!'

Someone was calling for Meeta from downstairs. Virender looked out of the window. Patricia, their neighbour, was standing at the gate.

'Meeta, I think Patricia has come to meet you,' Virender told Meeta.

Meeta went downstairs.

Dayaram had already opened the main door.

'Hello, Patricia, how've you been? I haven't seen you for ...' Meeta was astonished to see Patricia crying.

'Hey, what's wrong Patricia? Why are you crying? Come here, sit down. Let me get you a glass of water.'

Meeta went to the kitchen to bring some water for Patricia.

After taking a few sips, Patricia seemed to cool down a bit, but she was still solemn. Her eyes were red from crying and her face looked puffy.

Meeta sat with her in silence, giving her time to take hold of herself.

Finally Patricia spoke, 'Auntie, I came here to give you these keys. I am leaving.'

'Where are you going? And where is Peter?' Meeta asked her.

'Peter has not come home for the past two days. I know, he must be with that girl.' Patricia started crying again.

'Which girl? What are you talking about Patricia?' Meeta asked, astonished.

'Auntie, Peter is having an affair with a girl. I myself saw the two of them coming out of DJ Mall a few days ago. When I asked Peter about her, he accused me of spying on him. I know, he wants to leave me because I cannot bear him children. He must have known that girl for a long time because the way they were laughing and talking to each other, they looked so compatible,' Patricia told Meeta, amidst sobs.

'Dayaram, please make some tea for all of us.' Virender called to their servant while coming down the stairs with Ravi.

'Hello Patricia, how are you?' Ravi extended greetings to Patricia whom he had known from his previous visits.

'Hi Ravi, hello Uncle.' That was all Patricia could manage through her tears.

'There seems to be some serious discussion. I think we will sit in the garden,' Virender said to Ravi.

'No, Uncle there is nothing to hide now. Peter is having an affair with another girl, so I am going back home to my parents in Chennai,' Patricia explained to Virender.

'And what makes you think that Peter is having an affair?' Virender asked Patricia, while sitting down on the sofa opposite her. Ravi also sat down beside him.

'Uncle, you know we have been married for the past five years, and we have no kids. Although Peter never said this to me, but he has always longed for a child. Recently I spotted him at DJ Mall with a young girl. When I accused him of having an affair with that girl, he refused to accept it. When I pestered him to tell me the truth, then day before yesterday he just went out of the house and did not return. I tried his mobile number but he is not picking up. I have called up all his friends, but he is not at any of their places. He must be staying with that girl. I know Uncle, Peter has ditched me for that girl. What option do I have now except for going back to my parents?' Tears started flowing down Patricia's cheeks.

Meeta patted her hand. In the meantime, Dayaram brought tea for all of them. It seemed to soothe Patricia's nerves a bit.

After drinking tea she handed over the keys to Meeta and said, 'Auntie, please give these keys to Peter whenever he comes back. Tell him I have stepped out of the way. He can bring his beloved home.'

'One second Patricia', said Virender placing his own empty cup of tea on the table, 'how can you be so sure that Peter is having an affair with that girl? She could be one of his colleagues or his client. When you accused him of having an affair with that girl, did he accept the allegation?'

> Before you get upset, put yourself in your partner's shoes. Seeing the situation from your partner's perspective might change your own

'No Uncle, but he didn't deny it either. He always maintained a stony silence. He would just go into a shell. Day before yesterday, when he came very late, I broached the topic again and he just kept standing there while I shouted at him. Then without speaking a single word he left me. Since then he hasn't come back. Obviously he does not have the courage to face me now that I have caught him redhanded,' Patricia said.

'But this is so strange Patricia. I met Peter last week at Mother Teresa Home and he told me that he was planning a surprise for your birthday. He seemed to be in a good mood,' Virender said.

'Today is my birthday. I think this is the surprise he wanted to give me. He is leaving me for good,' sobbed Patricia.

'You give me Peter's mobile number. Let me talk to him,' Virender asked Patricia.

Patricia wiped her tears and quietly gave him the number. Virender tried the number from his mobile. After talking to Peter for some time, he placed the phone down and turned to Patricia. 'Patricia, Peter is on his way home. He has asked you to stay here for some time. Come, I'll show you my roses in the meantime.'

Virender took them all out to the garden.

The cool breeze and the beautiful red roses in the garden were refreshing. Patricia too seemed relaxed when a car drove into the portico. Peter came out with a girl holding a bundle in her hand.

'She's the same girl,' Patricia whispered to them.

'Hello Peter.' Ravi stepped out to welcome Peter.

The two shook hands while Peter introduced the girl to them, 'Uncle, she is Alice, my colleague. Alice, meet my wife Patricia, Uncle Virender, Aunty Meeta and Ravi.'

'Hello. Happy birthday, Patricia. This is for you.' Alice handed over the bundle to Patricia who looked on dumbfounded. As Patricia took the bundle from Alice, her eyes opened wide with surprise. The bundle held a small baby girl who was sleeping blissfully. She looked at Alice, then at Peter unable to speak a single word.

Peter came forward and held Patricia by her arms.

'I know I have a lot of explaining to do. Let's go inside.'

As they all settled down on the sofa, Virender addressed Peter, 'First of all you have to explain your absence for the past two days.'

'I spent the past two days at Mother Teresa Home, completing all the formalities. Though I could have come back home but I was so hurt by the accusations Patricia had hurled at me that I decided to stay at their guesthouse till I got all the adoption papers signed.'

'Adoption papers! You mean you have adopted this baby... without even consulting me!' Patricia could not contain herself.

'Patricia, again you are getting me wrong. I wanted to tell you, but you were in no mood to listen to me. After that incident at the Mall, you hardly ever spoke to me in normal tone. Whenever I wanted to discuss you, you would either refuse to speak to me or broached that incident only, which infuriated me to no end. I wanted this baby to be your birthday gift and time was running out in these unnecessary arguments. So I decided to take the initiative on my own and adopted this six-month old baby from Mother Teresa Home with Alice's help. Alice and her husband had earlier adopted a baby boy from that home. So she was familiar with all the procedures and formalities. In fact, she was the one who suggested that I adopt a baby to keep you occupied at home while I was away the whole day long. Little did she know that her noble gesture in trying to bring you out of your depression would backfire and you will take her to be your rival. That day we had come after speaking to Mother Superior at the Home, who had readily agreed to let us adopt a baby girl, as you always wanted to have a girl child. On our way back home, Alice asked me to stop by at DJ Mall to do some shopping. I had intended to disclose this news to you as soon as I reached home. I didn't know that a different kind of storm awaited me there. Patricia, you have punished me for no fault of mine. What have I done to lose your trust? Have I ever betrayed you? I have always been yours and will always be.' Peter spoke with such emotion that all eyes watching him turned misty.

'Peter, forgive me please. It's all my fault. I forgot that in a marriage it is very important to have faith in each other. Alice is right. The empty days filled my mind with all sorts of ideas which proved hazardous to my marriage. But now I will be busy, very, very busy with my baby.'

Patricia kissed the child lovingly on her forehead. The baby smiled sweetly in her sleep, as if acknowledging her mother.

'And what about your husband...?' Alice nudged Patricia in a fun way.

'Yeah, now I have two babies to look after,' Patricia teased Peter.

Everyone laughed at her.

Ravi was dreamily looking at this happy family reunion. He could not help himself from reminiscing towards those early days of his own marriage.

Avi was not born then. Ravi had not established his own business at that time. He was working in an Export House. He used to go on tours quite often. Since Richa used to get bored sitting at home, Ravi would take her with him whenever he went on tour anywhere. But it was not always possible because she got bored there also, sitting in the hotel room while Ravi attended to his clients or meetings. In the meantime Richa got pregnant. Now it was impossible for her to travel with Ravi. As the initial euphoria of having another addition to the family died down, Richa started feeling lonely. She started pestering Ravi to either take her with him on tours or stay in town himself. Ravi was in a fix. During one such time, Ravi had to go to Chennai on an urgent business call. One of the female officers of the company accompanied him. Ravi did not tell Richa about this, as he had not attached much importance to this fact. It so happened that as they were travelling together, their mobiles got mixed up. Ravi took her mobile to be his and gave his own mobile to his colleague. When Richa called on his mobile, this lady picked up the phone thinking it to be her own phone. When she understood that it was Ravi's wife on the line, she came calling to his room to give him back his phone and take her own. But the damage was already done. Richa had assumed whatever her empty mind made her think. She imagined and contorted various stories of the affair between that lady and her husband. Ravi still remembers how he had solved that problem with great difficulty. He had to invite that lady officer and her husband for dinner to prove to Richa that there was nothing going on between them. But God forbid, if that lady officer had been unmarried, Ravi shuddered to think what would have been the fate of his marriage.

Ravi smiled to himself.

But that was not the end of the story. Recently, Ravi also got the taste of jealousy when he saw Richa coming out of her colleague's car that had come to drop her at night, as they were working late in the office. Ravi felt a pang of jealousy in his heart. Though by now he was mature enough not to broach such a sensitive issue to his wife without even enquiring about things, he could not help feeling jealous and could not control his mood swings. For many days, he remained in a bad temper leaving Richa to wonder as to what instigated it. Slowly, Ravi managed to cool down and did not question his wife on this pretext, though he never forgot that scene and always remained on the look-out for any sign of infidelity on Richa's part, which he found none. Luckily, Richa did not notice anything and their married life seemed to move at a steady pace.

Today, seeing Peter and Patricia, Ravi realised how important it is to have trust and faith between husband and wife to maintain a stable relationship. Ravi felt proud of himself to have such a loving and trusting wife and be able to share so many loving moments with her. They had their share of ups and downs, but love always triumphed.

Ravi was exhilarated and felt like calling up Richa just to tell her how much he loved her.

Ravi wondered, when he last said 'I Love You' to her!

NOT IN A LONG TIME.

Rather than fight or flight,
use crisis as a time for growth

❑❑

Chapter 6

Twinkle in her eyes

A sound marriage is not based on complete frankness; it is based on a sensible reticence

After a scrumptious lunch on a leisurely Sunday afternoon, all three of them decided to relax. While Meeta retired to her room for a nap, Virender went into his study for completing some pending work. Ravi spread on the couch in the living room and put on the television. He started surfing through the channels. One channel was showing some advertisements for work-out on machines. As Ravi was about to switch the channel, something caught his attention.

This was the advertisement for a treadmill. They showed a fat man first. Then he was shown working on the treadmill and finally he looked thin and fit. The treadmill reminded Ravi of Richa. God, what a fight they had when Richa was insistent upon buying that treadmill. They used to argue almost every other day until Richa bought that damned machine. Ravi smiled. That girl definitely knows how to have her way.

'A penny for your thoughts!!' Virender's voice broke Ravi's reverie.

Ravi was surprised to see his father out of his study so soon. He asked, 'You finished your work so soon?'

'Don't change the topic son. You were not watching fashion channel, and you are not a health freak that you would smile looking at this health machine. So it has to be something else. What's on your mind?' Virender quipped.

Ravi smiled again. He wouldn't mind sharing that episode with his father.

'Dad, remember after my marriage, how I had started putting on weight. My sedentary lifestyle, regular partying and craze for fried food were mainly responsible for it. You remember how you used to pat me on my paunch and laugh.'

'Of course, I remember. I also remember how hard Richa worked towards getting you back in shape,' Virender said.

'You saw only what was before your eyes but what went behind the scenes – I'll tell you today. I have always been a great foodie and Richa is a good cook. So I think this combination turned deadly and I started putting on weight at an alarming rate. One day I had some pain in my chest. The doctor said it was gas and gave me some antacid. This episode shook Richa badly. In that short span of time, she had imagined all sorts of things. She even thought this was the beginning of angina or some other fatal ailment. Now she was after my life to reduce weight. She stopped cooking all those tasty fried dishes. What was dished out to me was simple boiled food which tasted…yuck…..how could anyone, in his right senses, swallow it. I, somehow, managed for a few days without hurting Richa's feelings. I knew she had good intentions. But Dad, she has this fetish, that when she starts on something she just has to finish it in the best possible way. She can't leave a job half done nor can she deviate from the path she has chalked out. She is very rigid in that sense.'

Virender smiled. He could feel the love and pride for his wife hidden in Ravi's statement, but he chose not to comment at that moment.

'Dad, can you imagine, she would wake me up early in the morning to go for jogging. When I came back, I was served sugar-free tea. Breakfast would be a boiled egg, tea and some porridge. Lunch …boiled vegetables, dinner…again some grilled or boiled stuff. No parties, no eating out. Dad, it was getting too much for me. On top of that, my weight was not coming down as expected. My mood swings were getting from bad to worse. I became short-tempered. However, Richa seemed determined to achieve her target, completely ignoring the fact that it was I who was suffering because of her over-enthusiasm.

'One day, she showed me an advertisement of a nearby gym and asked me to go and join it. I refused point blank. I told her in clear terms that I did not care whether I was fat or suffered from heart disease. I wanted to live life fully till I lived. So she had better stop being a bully and mind her own business. My goodness, Dad, all hell broke loose that day. There were tears, there were accusations, there were threats ...and for three days, we did not talk to each other.

'As the time passed, I realised my folly. She was doing all this for my good and here I was behaving like an ...'

'...oversized nincompoop.' Virender completed the sentence for him and winked.

Ravi smiled and continued, 'So I thought I would go and apologise to Richa and make her understand that she should go a little slow and then maybe I will be able to cope up. Believe me Dad, I tried to amend things in the best possible way, yet instead of a hug or a smile or even a cup of honey tea, she offered me black lemon tea and a brochure for this treadmill which would cost me about twenty thousand bucks. In a manner of compromise, I agreed to buy that machine. Can you believe, she kept reminding me for many days that it was she who compromised by not making me join the gym but allowing me to work out on the treadmill in the cool confines of home!' Ravi said.

'But you did manage to lose weight, didn't you?' asked Virender. 'Today you look fit and energetic. You should be thankful to Richa. She has been your pillar of strength.'

'I agree Dad. But at times she goes overboard with her enthusiasm. I mean, it's my life, I should have a right to decide what to do with it,' Ravi said.

'No, Ravi, you are not alone now. Your life is linked with two other lives. They depend upon you for everything. Richa and Avi are not just your family; they are a part of your life. This is the reason why Richa worries about your health. You are much too precious for her. She might have come across as a dictator to you but her good intentions cover up for her non-flexible attitude.'

Virender kept quiet for a while then spoke again, 'I think any of us can act stubborn if the need arises. I remember, when you and Ritika were small, I decided to get both of you admitted to the same school so that you could be together and it's easier for your mother to monitor. But your mother had different ideas. She wanted Ritika to go to an all girls' school near our house. Though the school was good but it was a Hindi medium school and was nothing compared to the one I was planning to put you in. Every day, we would have arguments over this issue. Your mother's argument was that the school was nearby and a co-educational school might spoil the girl. I could not understand why she was talking like an illiterate person till one day I heard your mother talking to one of her aunts over phone. She was telling her how I was being so adamant and not letting her shift Ritika to that school as suggested by that aunt. Now I understood who had put these silly notions in her mind. I knew I had to take a stern stand and that too subtly if I wanted to keep my marriage going.' Having spoken all this, Virender kept quiet.

> Create an oasis of comfort, unconditional love and encouragement within an unpredictable and frequently disappointing world

Ravi looked at him expectantly, 'Why this suspense. Dad, tell me, what did you do?'

'I'll tell you on one condition that you will never disclose it to your mother,' Virender asked.

'Certainly not,' Ravi promised.

'I told your mother that if she did not concede to Ritika

studying in the co-ed school, I would put you in a boarding school in Nainital. Your mother thought I was joking and she just laughed it off. She knew I loved you so much and I would never even in my dreams think of putting such a small child in a boarding. She even went and filled up the form in that girl's school for Ritika. The next day, I packed your bags and mine and left for Nainital,' Virender said.

'But Dad, I have no memories of living in a boarding school ever. How old was I?' Ravi asked.

'What has age got to do with it son, when you never ever attended boarding school. I took you to your Dadi's place. I stayed there for two days, left you with Dadi and Dada and came back to Delhi. Your mother was in a bad shape. She never expected this from me. At first, she was angry. She shouted at me for leaving her small child in the care of strangers. She told me to bring her son back immediately. When I reminded her of my clause, she didn't utter a word but within two days, Ritika got admission to that co-ed school and you followed her after I brought you back from Dadi's place,' Virender finished.

'Wow, Dad, great mind at work. Mom must be very, very angry at you when you told her this secret mission of yours,' Ravi asked.

'Told her! Are you out of your mind? Son, there are some things in life which should be left unsaid. I never told Meeta about this episode, neither did your Dadi or Dada,' Virender said, confidently.

'But why, Dad? She would have understood.'

'I know she would have, but then her faith in me would have been shattered. You know Ravi, in marriage it is very important to have faith in each other. So I decided to keep mum,' Virender added.

'And what if I already knew it,' Meeta's voice startled both of them.

She was standing behind the sofa, listening intently to every word they spoke. A naughty smile played on her lips.

'What do you mean?' Virender asked, 'What did you know?'

'That well-guarded secret which you were so proudly sharing with your son just now. I know Ravi never went to boarding,' Meeta said and came forward to sit on a sofa near Ravi.

'But how did you come to know? Ma told you or Dad...?' Virender was shocked at this discovery.

'Neither ... in fact the very person whom you least expected told me. Your dear son, who has been smiling at your secret right now, gave away your secret at that time. In your moment of triumph, you forgot to prepare your innocent son properly about the boarding school. Everything became crystal clear to me when one day I was asking him about his boarding school and he, in all his innocence, told me that it was a big house, just like Dadi's house and there was Dada and Dadi also. It didn't take me long to put two and two together,' said Meeta.

'Then why didn't you say anything to me all these years?' Virender asked her quietly.

'Why! ...a good question indeed. Well, I am not a fool, Veer. By that time I had realised that I was at fault. I had listened to an orthodox aunt of mine and was about to spoil my daughter's future. You saved me from making a wrong decision. Do you think I would have embarrassed you by demanding an explanation from you? Never! In fact, you gained more respect in my eyes after this episode. I knew I could always depend upon you for bringing me to the right path whenever I went wrong,' Meeta said with emotion.

Ravi looked at the twinkle in his mother's eyes. It was unconditional love and respect for his father. It takes a lot of patience, endurance and caring attitude to gain that kind of respect from your life partner. His father had earned that twinkle.

When did he see such a twinkle in Richa's eyes?

NOT IN A LONG TIME.

A man far too busy to care for his health, is like a mechanic who is far too busy to care for his tools

Chapter 7

Excuse me!

The trouble in marriage often starts when the man is so busy earning his salt that he forgets his honey

It was Monday morning. Ravi had his conference scheduled for 11 o'clock. Virender offered him lift which he gladly accepted. It was almost 10.30 a.m. when they finished their breakfast and set off to work. Meeta came out to see them off. Their car drove out of the portico.

The roads were pretty crowded with office-goers rushing to work in what ever means of transport they could afford. Ravi and Virender were discussing the reforms introduced by the Government in the Budget and how far they were successful when suddenly Ravi pressed hard on the brakes. The car came to a screeching halt. There seemed some sort of commotion ahead of them. Ravi got down to check what was it all about. A Maruti car had crashed into a Santro. Now the owners of the two cars were involved in a verbal fight accusing each other of careless driving. A crowd had gathered there and they were trying to pacify them. Meanwhile, a few abusive words had escaped the driver of Maruti car and the driver of Santro was busy trying to extract an apology from him. Within a matter of few minutes, they forgot all about their cars and the fight turned into a matter of personal prestige.

Ravi came back to his car. Luckily, there was a diversion close by. He turned the car in that lane and moved ahead.

Virender, who was till now sitting in the car, asked Ravi as to what the matter was. Ravi related the entire episode to his father who smiled nonetheless.

Seeing his father smiling, Ravi spoke again, 'Really Dad, it's so funny. You know these people started off with banging their cars and by the time police came they seemed to have forgotton all about their cars. They were busy fighting over something totally different.'

Virender nodded, 'It happens. One thing leads to another and the outcome is something we would not have imagined even in our wildest dreams. We read about road rage, and how people even kill each other over a simple fight. The reason behind this is that while fighting we argue and arguments lead to switching topics. This happens in homes too. Something like this happened last month with me.'

'I think it was a Monday – the busiest day in the office. Your mother asked me in the morning to bring a medicine for her while coming back from office. It was her blood pressure medicine, which she has to take every day. Due to my very tight schedule in the office, I forgot to bring her medicine. Unfortunately, that night I reached home quite late too. When she asked me about the medicine, it came back to me. By that time all the medical stores in the area were closed. I simply told her that I was busy with meetings in the office, so I forgot to bring her medicine and that I would get it the next morning from the nearby chemist shop. But she insisted that she had to have the medicine now itself. I was very tired, still I tried to keep my cool and make her see reason.

'But she was in no mood to listen. She followed me to the bedroom where I was about to change the clothes. First of all, she chided me for being so careless. She said: 'If you were not bringing the medicine you could have called me up. I would have gone to the market myself and bought the medicine. You always do this. Last time, I told you to bring orange juice for me then also you came back empty handed. You don't care for me in the least bit. Your memory is becoming atrocious. You buy things and leave them at the shop. All that you ever worry about is your office.....' On and on this went for a long time. Now this was getting out of hand. Finally, I too lost my cool. By now she was arguing over things which happened long ago. These things had no connection with our present-day situation. Still the argument went on, with me also joining the brigade without thinking of its repercussion. We kept switching topics from medicine to juices to grocery to clothes, to car parts – the list was endless.

'For the next half hour, we both argued over silliest of things while she stood there with the bowl of *dal* in one hand and serving spoon in another and I sitting on the edge of my bed with my coat and trousers off, my tie hanging from my neck, buttons of my shirt opened and my socks still on my feet. The argument also switched channels. We moved on from my atrocious memory to her never-ending gossips. We kept following each other from topic to topic, when I suddenly stopped, 'Wasn't this fight over a medicine? Then why are we fighting over your kitty parties and my official meetings.' This shut her up immediately. She banged the spoon into the bowl and stormed out of the room. Now as I sat quietly contemplating over the situation, I realised why Meeta was behaving in such an absurd manner. Her blood pressure must be shooting up. She must have wanted the medicine to keep herself away from those headaches that were very painful. Little did she realise that this unnecessary argument must have already led to an increase in her blood pressure by now. I realised my folly. I shouldn't have been so careless. I immediately put my clothes back on and rushed to a distant chemist who opened 24 hours. It took me half an hour to bring her medicine. By the time I came back, she was already feeling sorry for arguing with me unnecessary, but when I gave her the strip her face brightened up. I could see that it

> You will never put out a fire if you keep adding fuel to fire. You will never resolve an argument if you keep adding grievances

was not the medicine which brought that glow on her face, the glow came from the feeling that someone cares!'

What Virender said set Ravi thinking. He and Richa too often had arguments like this. They would start off with something else and by the time their argument ended, they would have analysed their entire married life and judged each other critically a hundred times over.

'But how to overcome this problem, Dad. We, too, face the same problem. The truth is that such arguments leave a bad taste in the mouth. It takes us days to recover from such fights,' Ravi asked his father.

'Ravi, you cannot stop arguing completely because you are two individuals living under the same roof. You have been brought up differently, your ideas are different and you treat life in your own individual style. So conflicts are bound to arise in married life. It is really strange how in a fit of anger we shoot such piercing words towards our partner that we forget how much we love and care for them. To keep the situation under control, all you have to do is finish your argument as soon as possible. This will help you in not divulging into other problem areas of your relationship and then you will not plunge deeper into unnecessary arguments. Do not let your past muddle up with your present. Got it.' Ravi nodded as Virender finished his monologue.

'Turn right from here Ravi, your conference hall is in that next building,' Virender pointed towards a red building ahead.

Ravi stopped the car. He picked up his briefcase from the back seat while Virender took over the wheel of the car. 'Call me up when you are free. Either I'll come or I'll send my office car to pick you up.'

Ravi nodded and waved to his father as he drove off.

Ravi turned around and started walking towards the conference hall when his phone rang.

It was Richa.

'Hello, how are you?' Richa's voice sounded so close he could even smell her musk perfume around him.

Oh, how he missed her!

'I'm okay. How are you? How's Avi?' Ravi tried to keep his tone normal. What had father said ...do not let past muddle with present! Let bygones be bygones.

'Dad told me you are coming to Bangalore on the 16th. Have you booked your tickets?' Ravi asked Richa.

'Yeah. I am taking the morning flight,' replied Richa.

There was a pause.

Neither of them seemed to think of anything to say. It was like a barrier which had been placed between them. Who would be the first to cross it?

'Ravi...'

'Richa...'

They both spoke together and then went silent waiting for the other person to complete the sentence. Finally Ravi mustered the courage to speak, 'Richa, I am sorry. I came away without telling you. But I was so angry....'

'Forget all that Ravi. We were both at fault. Even I behaved like an immature person. I am sorry too. But soon I am coming there and we will make up for these past few days.'

Ravi felt as if a big burden had lifted off his chest.

'Oh Richa, I love you.' He whispered in the phone.

'So do I, Ravi, so do I.' Richa said. Ravi could feel her breath in her husky voice.

There was a flight in his step as he climbed the stairs towards the conference hall. He decided to take the stairs than the elevator. He wanted to bask in the glory of his newfound happiness.

When did he feel so happy before?

NOT IN A LONG TIME.

The bonds of matrimony are like
any other bonds—they mature slowly

Chapter 8

Talk to me

You don't need to be on the same wavelength to succeed in marriage. You just need to be able to ride each other's waves

'Hello, Dad. I am glad you could get away early from office,' Ravi said to his father as he sat in the car.

'How was your conference?' asked Virender, as he drove down the road.

'It was good. They introduced us to the latest trends in the global market. The presentations as well as the speakers were excellent. I, too, have to make a presentation on the last day of the conference,' Ravi explained.

'Care for some coffee, son. This place serves some excellent brew.' Virender asked Ravi as he stopped the car in front of Coffee House.

Ravi nodded. He always loved spending time with his father. He was so full of life, jubilant and helpful all the time.

They entered Coffee House. It was like entering a different world altogether. The ambience was mesmerising, though completely devoid of any gaudy decorations. A sweet bitter aroma of coffee hovered around in the atmosphere.

Coffee House was almost full. Virender spotted a place in the far corner. He motioned to Ravi who followed him there. Most of the tables were occupied by couples, who were busy among themselves with not a care for the world around them.

There were groups of intellectuals who sat there discussing the present political scenario, economic policies, literary pursuits and any other topic under the sun. No one gave a damn to who sat on the next table.

'They serve better coffee than your ***Baristas,*** said Virender, as they took their place at the corner table. 'There are no fancy coffee flavours like *mochas, crème* or *cappuchinos* that your generation boasts of. What they serve here is just simple coffee made with freshly ground beans. And I assure you, you won't miss any of those flavours once you get the hang of this coffee.'

Ravi smiled. Within his heart his father was still a traditional Indian who loved his country with all its curries, flavours, fights and flights. The waiter came to their table and they ordered for two coffees and cheese sandwiches.

As they sat there waiting for their order to be served, Ravi told his father about Richa's phone call. 'It felt as if nothing had happened between us. We were just a phone call away and we kept waiting for the other to take the first step. I wish I had listened to your advice and called her that night. She has again beaten me,' Ravi told his father.

His father looked at him intently and then after a while he spoke, 'Life is not a game Ravi where you take turns. She called you because she loves you. Why do you feel that she has defeated you. She has just taken a step towards you, to which you reciprocated. If you hadn't..., I shudder to think what could have happened. You remember Kishan uncle....'

'Yeah, the one who lived in Dehradun.' Ravi recalled.

'Yes, his son Ruchit...' Virender stopped as the waiter brought their coffee and sandwiches.

Ravi took the first sip from his cup of coffee. It was bitter, yet certainly very different from what he was used to having. He could feel the warmth seeping through his body. It was a lovely feeling.

Virender took a bite of the sandwich and sipped coffee from his cup. 'I can see you liked your coffee.'

Ravi smiled.

'I was telling you about Kishan uncle's son. Kishan is my cousin. He had two sons. The elder one Ruchit joined his family business early in life. Naturally, when the son starts earning then parents think of his marriage. So they got him married at a tender age of twenty-two to Suruchi, who was a good four years younger to him. Both were young and somewhat spoilt kids of rich families. They went to Europe for their honeymoon. Even when they came back, most of the time they were out visiting relatives. The first three months of their marriage were bliss. They were so much in love with each other that they took no notice of other things.

> Respect and honour your partner. Keep the communication channels open. Closing them would lead you to a dark tunnel which would seem never-ending

'Slowly their dream world came crashing down. Ruchit had to work hard to make up for the loss in his company due to his absence. Suruchi, on the other hand, stayed mostly at home while Kishan would come late at night. Suruchi was an outgoing girl. She was not used to sitting in the house for long. She joined kitty parties, clubs and started enjoying life on her own. Ruchit never stopped her from doing anything. But their different routines had sort of put a rift in their relationship.

'One day, Ruchit's meeting got cancelled. Ruchit decided to surprise his wife. It was six in the evening. He knew she would be at the club at this time. He drove straight to the club. He could not find his wife at the usual place. He tried to ring her on her mobile but it was switched off. Having enquired from all the possible places, he went back home hoping to find here there. She was not there either. A suspicion filled his mind and slowly he started cooking up imaginative situations which pointed towards his wife's infidelity. Though he had no proof, yet he sort of convinced himself that there could be no other explanation, when he saw her entering the house looking pleased as a plum.' Virender stopped to take another sip from his cup.

'Finding him home, Suruchi asked him as to what brought him back so early. Ruchit felt as if he saw a shadow pass her face on seeing him home unexpectedly. His suspicion took root and he asked her where she had been without telling her that he had already found out about her absence from the club. To which, Suruchi simply told him that she was at the club. This was the last straw. Ruchit could feel anger burning his body, but he controlled himself. He remained awake the whole night.

'When he woke up in the morning, he seemed to have decided on something. He asked Suruchi to come for a drive with him. Suruchi readily agreed. They drove down the hills towards dense forest area at high speed, where Ruchit's car banged into a huge cluster of trees. Ruchit jumped out of the car. Luckily, the car did not catch fire, but Suruchi was badly hurt. Hearing the loud banging of the crash, many people from around the areas gathered there. Ruchit and Suruchi were brought to a hospital. Ruchit was given first aid as he was not badly injured, just a few bruises here and there, but Suruchi was kept in the ICU. Ruchit was shocked when the doctors told him that his wife was pregnant and that she had a miscarriage due to the accident. Being a small town, it was the same hospital where Suruchi's gynaecologist also visited. It was she who solved most of the mysteries for Ruchit. She told him that Suruchi had come for a pregnancy test on the previous day. She had the report with her. Two days later, when Suruchi came to her senses, she asked for Ruchit. She told him that she lied to him about going to the club. In fact, she had gone for the pregnancy test. She requested him to find out from the doctor about the report though she wanted it to be a surprise for him, but now the situation was different. She gave him a weak smile while he held her hand quietly.

'Ruchit came out of the ICU with tears in his eyes. How could he tell his wife that this accident had not only aborted her pregnancy but also made her incapable of ever conceiving again. If only he had not been so foolish and bided his time. Another day more, and they would have been on seventh heaven, waiting for the arrival of their first-born after nine months. If only Suruchi had told him; if only he had not been so impulsive; if only this accident had not taken place.... Ravi, there were so many ifs but sometimes life becomes such a miser that it does not give you another chance to amend your mistakes. The damage was already done. All Ruchit could do now was repent and cry for his foolish behaviour.'

Virender finished his coffee in one gulp.

Seeing his son sitting quietly like a statue, he shook his hand, 'Hey Ravi, it's all right now. All this happened six months back. Suruchi is fine now. They have now reconciled to the fact and have decided to adopt a child from an orphanage.'

'I didn't want to upset you. All I wanted to emphasise was the fact that there should be trust and understanding between the couple. And that comes from communication. Cutting the communication or severing the links to reach each other is the biggest mistake any couple can ever make. Today Richa has taken the first step and touched your heart. Next time it should be you who reaches out to her. This will make your marriage strong and you will last longer than others.' Virender winked at him.

As Virender got busy paying the check, Ravi sat back thinking about Richa. How he missed her now. His body longed to feel the softness and warmth of her body. His arms longed to embrace her and give her the warmest and longest hug of her life.

When did he last feel such emotions towards Richa and this longing to hold her in his arms?

NOT IN A LONG TIME.

A trust fund is no substitute
for a fund of trust

❑❑

Chapter 9

My money – your money, honey

Maturity does not come with age, but begins with the acceptance of responsibility

Four days passed in a jiffy. 16th November dawned on Ravi with the fragrance of roses. He felt elated, with a song in his heart. This was the same kind of excitement which he felt before meeting Richa in the initial days of their courtship.

Richa's flight was due at around 11 in the morning. Ravi was getting ready when he heard some commotion downstairs. He came out of his room and looked down the balcony. Lakshmi, their part-time maid, was sitting on the carpet sniffing and speaking loudly, while Meeta sat on the sofa listening to her. Ravi went back to his room, thinking it to be some women's matter, and started getting ready. After some time, he went down for breakfast. Lakshmi had left by then. All the loud noises of sobbing and sniffing had already stopped.

There was *alu-poori* and *lassi* for breakfast. Ravi sat down beside his father and pulled a plate. Meeta was busy serving warm *pooris* to Virender.

Ravi asked his mother casually, 'What happened, Ma, why was Lakshmi crying?'

Meeta placed a warm *poori* in his plate and then sat down beside him.

'Oh, it's the usual thing in their house. Her husband is a

drunkard. He not only spends his entire salary on liquor but he keeps on taking money from Lakshmi too. This time Lakshmi hid the money from him and lied to him that she had no money. But he was wiser. He started beating her and finally managed to extract all the money from her. Poor thing, she was crying at her fate. She herself is such a hardworking, honest woman. I don't know why she is putting up with such a man when she is bringing up her family literally single handed. He does not help her in any way. A man good for nothing.' Meeta concluded in anger and went inside the kitchen to get some more *pooris* for them.

'You know Ravi, there was a girl in my office. Her name was Rachana. She was a freelance artist. One day we came to know that she had committed suicide. It was a big blow for all of us because she was such a good-natured person. Later on we came to know that she had a big row with her husband the night before she committed suicide. Her husband was an executive in a bank. Though he earned a good pay packet, he was a spendthrift. He had this bad habit of gambling and used to lose large sums of money in it. They had recently renovated their flat, so most of Rachana's savings were spent on it. That day Rachana needed some money for running the house and for renovations too. She asked her husband to give her some money. Little did she know that he had lost a big hand just the night before! He had lost not only his entire salary, but took out all the money from their joint account too. When Rachana got to know of this, she confronted her husband. Though she was seething with anger she tried to keep her cool. But since guilty, her husband felt extra pricky and refused to answer any of her queries. He had also had a peg too many, at that moment, in order to forget his worries. In a bout of anger and frustration, she asked him as to who was he to

> Do not let your preconceived ideas of gender roles determine the respect you give to your partner. Form a mutual admiration society

spend all the money that she had earned with hard work. Hearing this, he started abusing her, calling her names and pointing fingers at her honour. In a state of depression, that night, Rachana ended her life. Her husband came out of his drunken stupor the next morning and was repentant but unfortunately, the damage was already done. It was something beyond repair. How could he bring her back from the clutches of death?

'If only he had valued her presence while she was still alive. If only he had valued the money and their relationship – their life would have been different.'

Virender had finished his breakfast. He was about to get up when Ravi spoke, 'You know Dad, something similar happened with us too. Some time ago, my company was facing a cash crunch. Many payments were in the pipeline but they were not coming through. I needed cash urgently to buy raw material. Richa had been already in the job for three-four months by then. Her salary was going into our joint account. First, I thought of taking out the money without even telling her. I knew I would be able to put it back as soon as my payments were through. But I don't know what stopped me from doing this. Instead, I told her that I needed a certain sum of money and if it would be all right if I withdrew it from her salary. Dad, I didn't know she would feel so happy for having asked her permission. She signed the cheque for the entire amount. It amused me so much because being a joint account, I could have signed the cheque myself. She was like a child who felt elated at having received so much attention,' Ravi laughed at the memory.

Virender too laughed loudly. He said, 'You did the right thing. Everyone needs recognition. In life, always remember to put yourself in the other person's shoes before acting in haste. Just think how you would have felt if Richa took out the money without telling you.'

Ravi nodded.

'I'm sure you had a lovely time after that,' Virender asked.

'Oh, groovy. She basked in the glory for quite some time and to tell you the truth Dad, I too was happy seeing that glow on her face. Really Dad, how these little things matter so much in life!' Ravi quipped.

Just then Meeta came in from the kitchen with another plateful of *pooris* for them. Looking at the smiles on their faces she asked them, 'What are you two looking so happy about?'

'Oh, we were discussing your *pooris*. They are so round and fluffy...the yummiest things on earth. They are so precious. They are like a treasure to us. We should do something to give them their due recognition...' Virender winked at Ravi, who gave a throaty laugh at his father's funny bone.

Knowing the ins and outs of her husband, Meeta knew that he was pulling her leg. She gave a stern look to both of them and said, 'If you are so fond of them then you two better have a few more and you have to finish them now,' saying so, she was about to place a few *pooris* in their plates when Ravi stopped her and pushed her down on the chair beside him. Then he told her the story of him and Richa which he had narrated to his father a few minutes ago.

Meeta smiled and patted him on his back, 'Good son, you set a good example by not being the typical MCP. Treat your wife with respect and at par, and you will find your married life much happier and enjoyable.'

Though a big boy now, Ravi felt as if he was being praised by his parents as they used to do when he brought home a trophy from school.

It was a feeling of elation which enveloped him completely. He had not experienced such exhilaration before.

NOT IN A LONG TIME.

We act as though comfort and luxury were the chief requirements of life, when all that we need to make us happy is something to be enthusiastic about

❑❑

Chapter 10

A secret we share

*Don't **help** with the housework, rather **share** the daily chores. Your home, children, pets, and so on are joint responsibilities*

It was almost eleven when they reached the airport. It was a Saturday and both Ravi and Virender had the weekend off.

Richa's flight was on time. As she came out with Avi, Meeta's eyes filled up with affection. Meeta was very fond of both of them, although Richa was not her choice. Ravi and Richa met through a common friend. As their friendship grew, they started liking each other. Earlier, Meeta was shocked to learn that Ravi was serious about Richa because in her heart she had chosen her friend's daughter to be her daughter-in-law. But her desire was a closely guarded secret for her. She never mentioned it to anyone. When Ravi first told her about Richa, she felt heart-broken. It seemed as if her son had betrayed her. But after some mulling, realisation dawned on her that she was being unfair. How was Ravi to know of her secret desire when she had never even disclosed it to him? So she met Richa with an open heart.

Meeta liked the girl instantly. Richa was a charmer. She was so simple and loving that Meeta found no reason to complain. As soon as Ravi got a job, the two were engaged with the consent of their parents. Marriage followed soon after. Initially, all of them stayed together in Delhi. Those days were so much fun. Meeta was like a good friend to Richa, and not the strict mother-in-law as portrayed in most of the films. Richa, too, reciprocated with similar love and gave due respect to her. Their relationship grew stronger when Avi was born. Meeta was in Bangalore at that time. They had shifted there due to Virender's new job. Meeta came to Delhi for Richa's delivery. She stood by her side throughout. Richa had filled the gap in her heart which was created by the absence of Ritika. Meeta's world revolved around Avi. It broke her heart when she had to leave him to go back to Bangalore. Though distance and busy schedules had kept them apart physically but Meeta knew she was the same Richa whom she had come to love so dearly.

Meeta came back to the present. Richa was touching her feet. Meeta hugged her lovingly. As Avi also bent down to touch her feet, she collected him in her arms and picked him up. She planted a number of kisses on his tender cheeks till he stopped her and planted a huge kiss on her forehead and said, 'Dadi, I love you.' All of them started laughing. Their little bunny had grown up. He acted just like his father – her son Ravi.

Meeta held Avi by hand and moved ahead of Richa and Ravi with Virender towards the car. They decided to keep slightly ahead giving the two of them some time together. Avi's innocent chatter had them into peels of laughter.

Richa looked at Ravi who was also looking at her. It seemed there was nothing unsaid between them. Quiet vibes seemed to flow between them. Ravi held Richa's hand in one and started pushing the luggage trolley with the other hand. His strong fingers felt tender on her hand. Richa felt something stir inside her. Was there ever a fight between them? Everything seemed as before. Was this the power of true love that people boast about? A smile played on her lips.

Soon they reached the car. Meeta, Virender and Avi were already sitting in the car. As Ravi put the luggage in the car's dickey, Richa sat beside Avi and Meeta on the back seat. Ravi sat in the driver's seat and the car started rolling on the road.

It was a homecoming of sorts. The house started reverberating with fun and laughter. After they freshened up, Dayaram made tea for everyone. There was still time for lunch. Avi went out to play in the garden with Dayaram. Virender and Ravi sat down on the computer in the study since Ravi had to prepare a presentation for his seminar.

Meeta and Richa sat in the living room catching up on all the news about each other. Meeta was careful not to broach the topic of Richa's tiff with Ravi. She enquired about her job and how she was managing home and her job simultaneously. Richa's answers were forthright. She never hid anything from Meeta, who was more like a mother to her. Richa considered herself lucky to have such an understanding mother-in-law.

It was not long before the much avoided topic came up accidentally. Meeta was enquiring about Avi's school when the matter of him attending the crèche came up.

'Why Richa.... why have you put such a small child in a crèche? Ravi told me that he could manage him but you did not want Avi to leave the crèche,' asked Meeta.

'Ma, I have never been in favour of Avi going to the crèche, but circumstances are such that I have no other choice. When Ravi got this big order which required him to travel a lot, we had put Avi in a crèche with mutual consent. Luckily this place is near our house. It is run by an old lady who believes in quality and not in quantity. She looks after Avi well and Avi has also adjusted with the environment there. It's a cozy house with only a few children, all of Avi's age group. Since I started going to office, I have changed six maids Ma, and every time Avi took a long time to adjust to them. By the time he would adjust to the maid, she would leave.'

'I agree Ravi has his office in the basement but his factory is far off. He keeps shuttling between his office and factory. He cannot keep an eye on the maid all day long. Then what's the guarantee that the maid will not mistreat Avi in his absence. Secondly, when it comes to finding a new maid, Ravi washes his hands off the entire matter. According to him, he has no time for such things. So I have to take leave from the office and stand in the queues of the placement agency to find a good maid. I hate being at the mercy of these placement agencies. They charge so much and then the maids they provide are pathetic. I was getting sick of this routine,' Richa said with a scorn.

'I know Ravi has been blaming me for not taking Avi out of the crèche, but you tell me Ma, Ravi's business is expanding, what is the guarantee he will not get another order which requires him to travel? What will I do then? It was all well until I was a homemaker. I could devote all my time to home and Avi. But now I have a responsibility towards my employers too. How can I keep taking leave so often? Unfortunately, Ravi doesn't want to understand this. This topic always causes conflict between us.' Richa was quite practical in her analysis. Meeta knew what Richa said was right from her perspective but she could not let Avi's future be spoiled like this. He deserved to enjoy his childhood under the protective wing of his mother.

> Different people say 'I love you' in different ways. Learn your partner's language so you can hear 'I love you' even when it is not said in the way you think it should be said

'I think it's about time, you gave up your job Richa. It's high time. You've already had some experience now. Let Avi grow up, then you can take up another job,' Meeta said.

'Ma, you know very well the circumstances which forced me to take up this job,' Richa asked her.

Meeta nodded. She remembered clearly when Richa had called to inform her of her decision to take up a job. She was crying on the phone, 'Ma, I don't know what's got into Ravi. He thinks I am good for nothing. He feels I sit at home the whole day and watch TV or gossip with my friends. The wives of most of his colleagues are working. He feels that I am no match to them. They are somewhat superior to me. He feels if they can manage home as well as work, why can't I? But Ma, why doesn't he understand, their children are old enough to manage themselves. But Avi is small. I love my home and my baby.' Richa cried over phone while Meeta listened to her in stunned silence.

What had come over her son? Why was he being so harsh on the poor girl? Either he could not see or he was turning a blind eye to the problems all working ladies face in keeping a balance between home and work front. Not all that glitters is gold. Ravi was looking at the outer shine of their homes, what lies beneath it was unknown to him.

Meeta was thinking all this when Richa put her very emotions into words. Her voice rang in the phone, 'I have many friends who are working and I know how difficult it becomes for them at times, to manage home and job simultaneously. But Ravi feels all this is an excuse. He keeps pestering me to take up a job. He promises to help me as much as possible. But Ma, I know from experience that once he has his work before him, it overshadows every other thing in his life, including me and Avi.' Richa was sobbing now.

Meeta had felt sad. How she wished she could be with her daughter-in-law to ease her pain, the pain that was brought on by her own son. She understood Richa's craving for being a homemaker because that is the basic instinct of a woman. When she did not need to go out to work and she did not want to, then why should she...just because her husband fancies her to be a working woman? What's wrong with Ravi?

First Meeta then Virender tried to convince Ravi to stop being so stubborn but Ravi was so taken in by the charm of working ladies that he wouldn't give up. 'Of course,' he said, 'there was no pressure on Richa. If she didn't want to work, it's upto her but she was just wasting her education and losing out on a good opportunity.' He had even arranged for a good job for her in one of his friend's company. He felt that everything was being served to Richa on a platter. She would be foolish if she did not grab it.

Very reluctantly, Richa took up that job, mostly to escape Ravi's taunts. Meeta even offered to take Avi with her to Bangalore but neither Richa nor Ravi could imagine being separated from Avi. Till some time the arrangement worked fine. Richa's busy schedule now did not give her the luxury to talk at leisure with Meeta often, so there was much in Richa's life that Meeta had missed out in these past few months. That is why she was surprised when she found that so much had happened between the two of them.

Sitting before her as Richa cried her heart out to her mother-in-law, Meeta listened quietly to her daughter-in-law. For a long time the two of them sat discussing various issues till it was time for lunch.

'Dayaram..., Dayaram...*khana laga do*.' Meeta called out to the servant.

While they were having lunch, Meeta asked Avi, 'Avi, whom do you love the most – Mummy or Daddy.'

Avi said, 'Not Mummy, not Daddy. I love Dadi.'

Everyone looked at him in surprise.

'Why, Avi? Richa asked him.

'Because Dadi tells me stories. She makes hot Maggie for me,' Avi said innocently.

Meeta looked at Richa. Their eyes met. Meeta could see the pain in her eyes. She looked away and started serving food to everyone. After lunch, they moved to the living room while Richa took Avi to his room for his afternoon nap.

'Ravi...' as soon as Meeta started, Ravi knew instinctively that it had to be something related to Richa and Avi.

Oblivious of his thoughts, Meeta continued, 'Richa has proved that she has the potential to work. But she has to look after little Avi too. Don't you think she has some responsibility towards him? Why don't you let her resign from the job and look after her home?'

'Ma, she can quit any time she wants to but I'm sure she will get bored very soon sitting at home. Soon Avi will start going to a proper school. How will she while away her time then? She will again indulge in gossip and kitty parties and make my life miserable. I still remember how she would pester me to take her out every other day. When Avi started his pre-school, she would complain of getting bored so often. Most of her old friends are working and wives of my friends are working ladies. Richa has her own kitty group but I feel they are all fake. That is why I have always encouraged her to join office so as to keep herself constructively occupied. I even arranged for her job in my friend's office,' Ravi said with a sense of self-pride.

'You do not want her to leave the job because you feel she will get bored at home or you do not want her to leave the job because it will be like defying your orders?' Virender asked him curtly.

'Dad, what made you say that?' Ravi was surprised.

'Because this is what I felt when you were busy blowing your own trumpet,' said Virender.

'Dad...' Ravi tried to say something when Virender again cut him short.

'The truth is bitter, hurtful and cold...as always.... yet it cannot be denied. You started as a liberal modern husband, who believes in equal rights for both husband and wife. However, somewhere along the line you moved away from your predetermined path and turned into a mentor for your wife. Your self-esteem and your ego got a boost whenever you were told by others as to how different you were for not only allowing your wife to work outside the house but also no one could touch your generosity in the way you procured your good for nothing wife a job. Your false sense of pride would be shattered now if Richa gave up that job to look after her home and family. That is why you want her to continue even though she herself wants to remain a homemaker. How else will you boast to your friends of your liberal views? How else will you make her feel obliged to you? No wonder, you keep reminding her....' Virender would have continued but Ravi stopped him short.

'It's not true, Dad. I only want the best for her,' he seemed quite disturbed.

'Your father does not mean to hurt you, Ravi.' Meeta tried to console her son for she knew that her husband could be very harsh at times.

Just then Richa entered the living room having put Avi to bed. As she was about to sit beside Meeta, Ravi asked her,

'Richa, tell me, have I ever forced my decisions upon you. Was doing this job not your choice?'

For a moment, Richa was taken aback. Soon she regained her composure and said, 'Ravi, to be very frank, I took up this job mostly to escape your sarcasm and to prove to you that even I can do something in life. Now I am tired of this game. Nothing matters to me more than my child and my home. I am seriously thinking of quitting this job. Once Avi and... (pause) grow up, may be I will take up another job. But for the time being....'

Richa kept quiet but her face was flushed.

Meeta was the first one to pick up the clue.

'What do you mean by Avi and....Is there some good news Richa?'

Richa blushed and nodded.

Ravi sat there dumbfounded when his father gave him a pat on his head.

'What a dumbo you have produced Meeta. Congratulations, Richa. I hope this one takes after me. My grandson will be as smart as his grandfather is, not a dimwit as his father.'

'Why not a granddaughter! She will be just like me,' declared Meeta. Their faces were glowing with joy.

Ravi seemed to be in a trance as he kept staring at Richa, when his mother's voice shook him out of his reverie.

'Ravi, you can settle scores with Richa later. First listen to me. I have a suggestion. Richa will not work full-time now. She can design clothes as a freelancer, but she will operate from home. Better still, since you are both in the same profession why don't you let her work part-time for your own company. This way her talent will not go waste and she will be able to devote time to her family and home too.'

'Hey, why didn't I think of that before? Of course, she can work in her own company. Ma, you're a genius. You solved such a major problem in a jiffy.' Ravi suddenly brightened up. He seemed quite enthusiastic.

Meeta and Richa smiled at each other at this sudden show of enthusiasm from someone who had been sitting there some time ago as if hit by a cyclone.

Virender too smiled, 'So that settles it. Richa, are you comfortable with this arrangement?'

Richa nodded.

'Good. Now you people carry on with your little chit chat, but excuse this old man. I think I'll take a nap. Coming Meeta?' Virender looked at his wife as he got up to go to his bedroom.

Meeta took the lead and followed her husband.

'Why didn't you tell me before?' Ravi asked Richa when they were alone in the living room.

Richa told Ravi how she got her pregnancy test done last week and it was confirmed positive, yesterday only.

'Oh Richa, I am so happy for us and for Avi too. Now he won't feel lonely as he will have a companion to play with,' Ravi moved closer to Richa.

The truth seemed to have sunk in slowly. He seemed genuinely happy. He was trying hard to contain his happiness.

He held Richa's hand, 'Hey, let's go shopping tomorrow. We will buy some groovy clothes and toys for the young chap.'

Richa smiled, 'Ravi, this is just the beginning. We have a long way to go. The baby is not due till next nine months. So why hurry. We'll have lots of time,' Richa said, laughing at her husband's child-like enthusiasm.

'You are so right. We will have lots of time now for us and for our kids. I've been too hard on you, too rude and totally indifferent. Please forgive me Richa. Today you have made me the happiest man on earth. I want to make amends for my past behaviour. This news has brought a fresh lease of life for our relationship. I will always cherish these moments.'

He collected Richa in his arms. As Richa rested her head on his broad shoulders, Ravi felt a strange sense of peace and serenity filling his heart. He felt no longing, no fear, and no cravings now. He felt as if he was floating upon the waves of calm and tranquillity where Richa was his soul mate in every true sense of the word.

Ravi smiled to himself as he held his beloved close to him. When had he felt such contentment within his heart?

NOT IN A LONG TIME.

A happy man marries the girl he loves;
a happier man loves the girl he marries

❑❑

Chapter 11

Sparkling diamond ring

Remember that successful marriage depends on two things: finding the right person, and being the right person

The next few days passed in a jiffy. Virender and Meeta's house was filled with fun, laughter and joy. Their anniversary party was due on Saturday. The arrangements were going on in full swing. They had invited about fifty people for the party – all close friends and office colleagues. Naturally, Dayaram could not handle such a big gathering alone, so Meeta arranged for the caterers. Meeta and Richa sat together and decided on the menu and other arrangements for the day. They planned to set the dining area on one side of the lawn and seating arrangements were made in the other part of the lawn. The bar was in the drawing room, so arrangement for a small gathering around the bar was also required. The menu was a heady mix of Indian, Mughlai and Continental food.

Richa took the reins from her mother-in-law and went about the work in her usual calm and composed manner which Meeta always admired. While her son was a bit edgy – she remembered fondly calling him '*Phudku*' when he was small – her daughter-in-law was always the confident and dependable kind. Meeta smiled affectionately at Richa who was busy calling up the caterers and fixing up the menu with them.

While the two women in the house were busy with party arrangements, the men went about their work in a routine manner.

Ravi's conference was over by Friday evening. He and Richa went shopping for a gift for Virender and Meeta.

D day dawned with a beautiful sun smiling on Rose Villa. Virender opened his eyes as the warm sunrays touched his face lovingly. He looked to the other side of the bed, which was occupied by Meeta. It was empty. She must have gotten up by now. As Virender turned around to the side table to check the time, he found a small package neatly wrapped in pink folds.

'That's my Meeta.' Virender smiled to himself and started opening the package. It held a pair of diamond cufflinks. They looked bright and shiny. Virender smiled at this lovely present which was obviously from his wife. He reached out to his drawer to take out the gift for his wife which he had bought for her. It was not there. All woken up, Virender jumped out of the bed and searched his entire drawer, briefcase and the pockets of his coat which he was wearing last night. But the packet was nowhere to be found.

In desperation he decided to enquire from Meeta when suddenly the door to his bedroom opened. Meeta came in with his morning tea. She looked her bubbly self.

'Happy Anniversary!' she wished him as she handed him the tea cup.

'Yeah, same to you. That was a lovely gift which you gave me. Thanks.' Virender felt at a loss of words as he took the cup from Meeta and started sipping tea nervously.

When he looked up, he saw Meeta looking at him expectantly.

'Yes?' Virender knew she was waiting for the gift but he could not dare tell her that he had lost her gift. The expensive diamond and sapphire ring which he had specially bought for this day, was missing.

He looked at Meeta's fingers. Maybe she took it out and is wearing it now. She loved teasing him. But the ring was not there either.

He wanted to tell Meeta that he had lost the ring just like he had done on their fifth wedding anniversary.

Virender still remembered that day vividly. He had recently been promoted to the post of General Manager. Their daughter Ritika was three years old and Ravi was just born. Everything seemed to be going great for him. Like every year, Virender had planned to buy an expensive diamond ring for Meeta. This was one promise he had made to Meeta on their wedding night that he would give her a beautiful diamond ring, however big or small, on every anniversary.

That year they were not giving a party on their anniversary because Ravi was just fifteen days old and Meeta was still very weak. But that did not mean he could forego her promised gift.

> Make birthdays, anniversaries and holidays important. Celebrating these special days can be fun and romantic. Establish annual romantic traditions that you can look forward to year after year

As luck would have it the anniversary day dawned. Virender had a very important meeting scheduled for 8 o'clock in the morning. In his hurry to get ready, he forgot to wish Meeta in the morning. He remembered as he reached midway. He decided to call her up from the office. Unluckily for Virender, his day was so busy and his schedule so tight that he did not get even a single moment's respite to even call up Meeta, what to think of going to the jeweller's shop to buy the promised ring. By the time he finished off with his meetings and other office work, it was nearing ten in the night. Exhausted, he headed homewards only to find a cold dinner, uncut cake, his gift and a note from Meeta's brother, waiting for him at the dining table. It seemed his in-laws had come there to celebrate their anniversary and give him a surprise, but got the big surprise of their lives themselves.

The entire day came back to him in a flashback.

'Shit...shit...!' was all he could mutter as he remembered that he had neither wished Meeta nor bought any anniversary gift for her.

Just then the servant entered with a glass of water for him. He told Virender how everyone kept waiting for him and then went away without even having dinner.

Virender could not think of any excuse to be given to Meeta as he entered the bedroom. As expected Meeta was wide awake. And what a showdown they had after that. Virender still shudders to think of that day. It was not what Meeta had said or accused him of... it was the feeling of guilt which gripped him that was unbearable. He was a man of words. He had always kept his word. It was unthinkable for him to go back on his promise.

The next day saw both of them in a much gentle mood. Virender took the first step towards reconciliation and Meeta went ahead with it. Virender never wanted to repeat the episode. So he made Meeta promise that in future she be the first one to wish on their wedding anniversary and Virender will follow suit. Meeta agreed to her husband's suggestion thinking it might bring him on the right track. Little did she know that in the coming years it will turn into a tradition which she wouldn't mind following.

Since that anniversary, although Meeta was always the first one to wish Virender on their anniversary in the morning, on his part, Virender too never forgot to bring her that ring which she always looked forward to so keenly.

Virender came back to that present. Meeta was sitting beside him looking expectantly at him. Virender had made up his mind. No more pretences. He would tell her the truth. He moved closer to his wife and said in his deep, husky voice, 'Happy Anniversary, darling. I had bought your ring yesterday. But it seems I have lost it somewhere because I can't find it anywhere.' Meeta kept looking at him without showing any expressions or concern. This had Virender really upset. He felt as if Meeta did not believe him. He again emphasised his point.

Finally, Meeta spoke in a soft voice, 'What do you think, I only care for that ring and not for your feelings? I had made you promise that ring every year so that you would not forget this day which is so important in our lives. I am witness to the effort and pain that you take every year in remembering our anniversary and this is the biggest gift for me,' saying so she ruffled his tousled hair and gave him the biggest hug of his life.

Just then there was a knock on the door. Meeta got up and opened the door. Ravi and Richa were standing outside.

'Happy Anniversary, Mom and Dad,' they both said in unison.

'So where's your ring Ma. Let me see the latest design,' Ravi said with a twinkle in his eyes. He had been a keen witness to his mother's large collection of numerous rings in all these years.

'I've lost it but today I have earned something special. After all these years, today I have realised how deeply your mother loves me. I was always aware of her feelings for me but today she has understood my predicament even without my having to say it. She is my soulmate in true sense,' Virender said these words with emotion.

Ravi smiled and said to Richa, ' Richa, have you seen how loss of a diamond ring can make one so emotional. I don't think I can bear to see him so serious and emotional on such an important day like today.'

Richa giggled.

Ravi turned towards his mother. He gave her a big smile and opened his palm before her. It held a velvety red box.

Meeta clicked it open. There was a beautiful diamond and sapphire ring in it.

'Hey, that's the ring I bought for your mother. Where did you find it?' Virender was beside himself with joy on having found his lost ring.

'I found it in the car while coming back with you from office last night. It must have fallen from your pocket while driving home,' Ravi told Virender.

'Now, as a penalty, you will have to place this ring in Ma's finger and sing a romantic song for her,' Ravi spoke again as he picked up the ring from its box and handed it to his father. As Virender placed the ring in his wife's finger, a feel of affection swept through his body.

'*Ai meri zohra jabeen, tu abhi tak hai haseen aur main jawan...*' Virender started singing loudly holding Meeta's hand, who sat there blushing trying to pull her hand out of his firm grip. Her face was glowing with happiness and her eyes shone with the love for her husband.

Richa and Ravi smiled at each other.

Ravi pressed Richa's hand softly. As the duo clapped for Virender and his melodious song, Ravi realised it was time he also took his wife and their love and relationship seriously. Why was it that he could not show this kind of affection to his wife? He longed to share that kind of chemistry with Richa which his parents shared.

He remembered his courtship days. Those were the days when he crooned for Richa, trying to woo her.

When was it last that he ever sang a romantic song for Richa?

NOT IN A LONG TIME.

Don't let someone else create your world for you, for when they do, they will always make it too small

❑❑

Chapter 12

Laughter is the best medicine

One of the greatest assets to a good marriage is honesty, along with a sense of humour

The party was in full swing when Mr. and Mrs. Menon walked in. They were Virender's office colleagues. Virender introduced Ravi and Richa to them. Mr. Menon was a jolly person who could turn even the gravest situation into a humorous one. His laughter was contagious. He gave that loud throaty laugh which made the heads turn and soon people would gather around him listening to each and every word he spoke with full attention. He was a people's man in the true sense.

After drinks were served, the conversation shifted to the recent epidemic of dengue in Delhi and other parts of the country. Everyone gave their views and it was amazing how each one of them knew at least one person who had suffered from that dreaded disease.

As the snacks were being served, the conversation drifted towards simple virus or the cold virus, when Mr. Menon took centrestage. He went into a monologue as to how people behaved when they suffered from cold. His imitations were so real that people were in splits. As the mood was set, Mr. Menon went on with his simple analysis of common virus which had varying effects on different people. He gave the example of a family.

'It's in the air, they all claim, and suddenly the itching starts in your throat and body feels lethargic. Usually it begins with the youngest member of your family which in most probability is your school-going son who comes home one evening with a running nose and red eyes. The mother takes the temperature – it's 100° F. His happiness knows no bounds. Fever means no school, no homework – the excitement is akin to watching the Indo-Pak Cricket match.

The next day dawns, mom's poor Palu watches Cartoon Network the entire day. The bitter medicine is swallowed under the stern gaze of mother, but there is compensation too in the form of chocolates which he devours in tons, quite happily. His older teenaged sister Sweta watches him in anger but no chocolates come her way, nor is she allowed to switch the TV channel to her favourite MTV.

Disgusted, she walks back to her room and turns the volume of FM on a higher note.

Within minutes, a loud call from mother instructs her to lower the volume as poor Palu is having a headache. Cursing under her breath, she lowers the volume and smirks at the noise of Cartoon Network filling her room.

As Palu tries to stretch his four-day long convalescence to another day, father acts adamant. 'You have no fever, no running nose. So no more missing school. Off you go today. Here, take this medicine.' Another bitter dose of that horrible medicine is thrust down his throat.

'I think, I have got it too,' declares Sweta as she comes back from her college the next day. Her body feels sticky and her legs ache. Mother takes her temperature – its 102° F. Off to bed, no more college for three days – orders mom.

Strange how the teen mind works in exactly the opposite direction as the pre-teen mind. The teenager smirks, tries to make mother see reason – I can't bunk college....I have a very important lecture scheduled tomorrow..... in other words she would be missing all the visits to the favourite hangouts with her group.... but mom is adamant.

Teens have their own ways of going viral and coming out of it. Pop goes the antibiotic and the motionless, miserable teen protests meekly and mews like a weak kitten. Having not got her way, she does what teens do best – she sleeps for four whole days straight. Nothing can stir her eyelashes. Not even the loud noise of TV except for the occasional ringing of her mobile phone. On the fifth day, she wakes up fresh and raring to go. You would feel she had never been ill.'

> Laughter and loving go hand in hand. Laugh together at every opportunity and be sure to create plenty of love around you

There was a loud roar of laughter from the audience, who were listening aptly to Mr. Menon. Seeing the effect he had on his audience, Mr. Menon attacks the rest of the clan with vengeance.

'Now it's dad's turn. Remember, dads do not encounter virus as long as the kids have it. They have it at their leisure and that too, loud. The entire house reverberates with their sneeze or cough or a simple demand for tea or coffee. The best way to announce that he has caught it is by not shaving. His bristles speak louder than words. The teenager asks him before leaving for college 'Not feeling well Pa?' As he nods, she calls out to mom and off she goes with her duty done. Mom rushes to him touching his forehead showing her due concern, when he suddenly says, 'I don't think I have fever.' Within seconds, the thermometer is in his mouth.

'A mighty 101°F recorded on the mercury and he speaks heroically – I suppose, I had better get ready for office.

'Now mom has to take the initiative and tuck him in bed declaring: no office today. Father obliges without further protest. All he manages to say is 'I feel terrible. I think I'll sleep for a while.' Afternoon sees him back on the couch in front of the TV, watching a cricket match. His moaning has turned to hollering: Where's my tea.... Get me some coffee...! and so on.'

Richa looked at Ravi and smiled meaningfully while Mr. Menon continued. Everyone was enjoying it immensely.

'The second and the third morning are a replay of previous day's episode until the mother has had too much. She has a long talk with her kitty friends. The fourth morning sees mother put her kitty party plan into action. It's guaranteed to cure sick dad instantly irrespective of the fact that the cricket match is still being telecast on TV.

'I think, I've caught the virus too,' Mother says as she produces a convincing sniffle. She continues, 'My head is pain...' when suddenly father leaps out of his cozy warm bed as if it was on fire.

'I just now remembered, I have a very important meeting today. Thank god I remembered it just in time.' He is out of the house before you could say 'flu'. Mom is pleased with her strategy and plans a leisurely afternoon sojourn with her friends when suddenly her head starts throbbing. The quiet and empty house gives her the relief that she is on her own, when she came down with it.

'Thank God no more tantrums to be dealt with.. No more tea, coffee or Bournvitas to be made. She tries the thermometer. It shows 103°F. She pops in a few pills, calls up her friends for advice on some home remedies and then the bell rings. The maid has arrived. Mom squeaks, 'Oh my God, it's 12 o'clock, the house is in a mess. I haven't even cooked food.' As the maid works, Mom hums under her breath. She does her daily chores as well as those which she normally doesn't do because today she is entitled to not having to do anything. So the house is spick and span within minutes.

'Thanks to the virus, today she has wiped the dishes dry and placed them in their right place, she has put all the clothes in the washing machine. She has even cleaned the cobwebs and changed the bed sheet on her bed. She smiles at her spirit and energy even when she is running 103° temperature. The maid has left by now. After a quick bath, mom stretches her aching legs on the sofa … oooh what bliss. What more could she ask for …? She drifts into a deep, exhausted sleep. No dreams to disturb her deep slumber….zzzzzzzz.

'When Palu rings the bell at 3p.m. then mom opens her eyes. Gosh, it's so late. As she listens to umpteen stories of his day, she feels normal. A little light-headed, but no more aches. 'I'm fine,' she thinks and feels exhilarated… So sir, that's the story of virus in a household. But the secret of everyone having the same virus differently is yet to be known.'

Mr. Menon finished his monologue. There was applause from all around. After a hearty laugh, conversation resumed.

Ravi approached Richa, 'Why were you smiling?'

Richa laughed, 'I could see you in that Dad in Uncle Menon's story. Don't you behave in the same way when you are sick? Remember, when you had a meeting with the Batliwalas and you came down with fever. However much I tried to convince you but you just refused to shave. My God, you looked like a stubborn bear who refused to be tamed and when I told you the same, you got so angry that you went to the meeting in those bristles.'

Ravi too smiled, 'Of course I remember, what a sight I looked and how stubbornly I behaved! I think I expected you to show more sympathy than you did that day.'

'Not sympathy dear husband, you were looking for your mother's care and concern in me. What a scene you created that day. I was furious for hours after you left. But today, when I look back, it all seems so funny.'

'That's true Richa. We do so many silly things on the spur of the moment. Anger takes away our power to think rationally and reason things out. We act immaturely and then repent later when it's too late to amend. Such situations tickle our funny bone when we look back at them later, with a cool perspective.'

Virender's voice made them turn around.

'Isn't Mr Menon hilarious? He really has his way with words.'

Ravi and Richa nodded smilingly.

Virender picked up two glasses of orange juice and handed over to both of them. Then he picked up one for himself and raised it in toast – 'To Richa's health.'

Three of them cheered. Virender moved ahead leaving the cozy couple revelling in their past memories.

The sweetness of juice filled Ravi's mouth. He felt at peace with himself. When had he laughed like this before?

NOT IN A LONG TIME.

Getting married is easy.
Staying married is another matter

❑❑

Chapter 13

Happy days ahead...

Living together is involvement; being married is commitment

The party was a great success. The guests enjoyed every bit of it. By the time their last guest left it was almost midnight. Since they were all very tired, they retired to bed soon after.

Next day was a Sunday. No one was in a hurry. The house bore a quiet look when little Avi got out of bed and strolled towards his Dadi's bedroom. The door was slightly ajar. Both Meeta and Virender were snoring blissfully. Avi went towards Meeta's side and crept into her bed quietly. Meeta woke up when she felt the warmth of little Avi beside her. She picked him up in her arms. Avi snuggled close to her. Meeta kissed him on his nose. Avi smiled at her and returned her kiss by kissing her on her nose too. Meeta couldn't help smiling.

Holding him in her arms, she began humming a lullaby. Within minutes, he was fast asleep. But Meeta could not sleep now. Avi reminded her so much of Ravi's childhood. How she loved to cuddle little Ravi in her arms. She still remembered how Ravi also used to creep in beside her once Virender was asleep.

Memories of those days were pleasant but there was a dark lining in her silvery cloud. Those were the days when Ritika was five years old and Ravi was almost two. Ravi was very much attached to her. Although he played in his nursery throughout the day, he loved to creep in Meeta's bed at night. Meeta loved it. Being a mother, she loved to mollycoddle her little baby but

Virender had other views. He wanted his kids to be independent from their very childhood. He always made Ritika sleep in a separate cot when small and he tried to follow the same discipline with his younger son too. Although Meeta longed to keep her little babies under her wing like a protective mother, she could not disagree with her own husband who had no ill intentions behind this arrangement. She consoled herself by thinking on the lines that after all he was not sending the kids to boarding. He only made them sleep in a different room so that they learn to be independent.

Ritika always followed this regimen but Ravi was different. He refused to let go of his mother even after he was two years old. Seeing this, Virender became strict with him and forced him to sleep in his own bed. Little did he know that this was his own species he was dealing with. Ravi was as adamant as his father was.

After initial days of separation from his mother at night, Ravi started creeping in quietly beside his mother in the stillness of night. But this time Virender was prepared. He would immediately rush him back to his own bed. Meeta was a mute spectator to all this. However, she could not contain herself any longer when she found Ravi bedwetting at night. He would not spoil Meeta's bed if he slept with her, but if he were forced to sleep in his own bed at night, he would go on his bedwetting spree religiously.

Meeta could not bear her little baby turning into a psychological case. One day she revolted and there was a major showdown between Meeta and Virender. They tried to keep the matter from the kids, but kids have extrasensory powers and they can sense anything unusual. Ravi had seen Meeta sobbing when Virender stormed out of the room after the fight.

Strange enough, that night Ravi did not come to Meeta's room and slept blissfully in his own bed. Virender was as amazed as Meeta herself was. But …Meeta smiled to herself….she knew, her little baby understood her predicament. So to bail her out, he amended his own way.

Meeta gave a loving kiss to Avi and got up from bed. She reminded herself to tell Richa about this episode in Ravi's life so that it did not repeat in Avi's life too.

As Meeta came down the stairs, a sense of loneliness started filling her. The kids would be leaving tonight. These past few days were complete bliss. She had her house full of laughter and time passed effortlessly. With children back in their nest, she would again be alone in this huge house.

If only wishes were horses, she would wish that they all stayed together forever. She was missing Ritika too. Ritika had called up last night to wish them happy anniversary, but she wasn't sure when she would be able to come to India. Meeta let out a deep sigh as she picked up the tray with two cups of tea for herself and Virender, and a glass of milk for Avi.

The three of them were sitting in the garden when Richa and Ravi came down after a refreshing sleep. The cool breeze was blowing and warm sun felt soothing on the face. There was so much to talk and so little time left. After a while Ravi and Virender went inside to freshen themselves while Richa and Meeta sat there chatting thousand to the dozen.

Suddenly they saw a car pulling up in the driveway. A young man alighted from it and walked towards them. He wished Meeta and Richa good morning. Meeta motioned him to sit down. Then she introduced him to Richa. He was Rajat, Virender's assistant. He had joined office recently so Richa had not met him before.

Rajat had come there to get some papers signed by Virender. Meeta asked him to wait for some time and asked Richa to go and inform Virender about Rajat's arrival. As Richa went inside taking Avi along, Meeta offered Rajat a cup of tea.

As Rajat sat sipping sitting tea, he couldn't help admiring the comfortable interaction between Meeta and Richa. Unintentionally, he happened to mention it to Meeta.

'You two look so comfortable in each other's company. No one can say that she is your daughter-in-law. She looks more like your daughter. You must be a very loving mother-in-law.'

'Thank you, but half of the credit goes to Richa also. She is the loveliest gift my son could ever give me,' Meeta said with pride.

When she looked up, she could see a cloud hovering over Rajat's face as he sat there sitting with his cup of tea.

Meeta couldn't help asking, 'I don't want to interfere but is there something which is bothering you. Tell me, I am like your own mother. Maybe I can help you.'

> Accept the entire package that is your partner

Rajat hesitated at first then he made up his mind, 'No one can help me. I know I have landed myself in a big mess. But I think sharing my problem with you will surely ease the burden on my heart. Two years ago, I fell in love with a Muslim girl. When my mother came to know she made such a hue and cry of the whole matter that I had to abandon the very thought of marrying her. You see, my father died very young. My mother brought me up with great care and efforts. I could not bear to break her heart so I gave in and got married to a girl of her choice who belongs to our own caste. Radhika, my wife, is a sweet girl. She adjusted well in our house. As luck would have it, two months ago she came to know about my affair with that Muslim girl. Since then she has changed completely. She does not trust me at all. There are frequent fights between us. When my mother tried to intervene, Radhika snubbed her rudely. She even accused her of being a party to the whole affair. Today my home is like hell. Not in my farthest of dreams can I ever imagine my mother and my wife sitting together and talking so animatedly as you and Richa*ji* were doing. Even if I sit and talk with my mother, Radhika thinks that we are conspiring against her. I don't know how to make her understand that when I married her, I let go of my past and made a fresh beginning with her. I love her no less than that Muslim girl because of the love and affection she showered on me in the initial days of our marriage. But these past two months, since the revelation of my affair to her, have been pure torture,' Rajat's voice became heavy with the pain he felt. 'Today, when I saw you and Richa*ji* together, I longed to see my family also so loving and happy. Maybe that is why I could not hide anything from you. I really wish someone could give me a magic formula so that my wife comes back to her senses and we can all live happily like before.'

Meeta sat there quietly contemplating for a few seconds. When she spoke, her voice was calm and soothing, 'Rajat, the way I conceive your problem is that there is some misunderstanding between you and Radhika due to communication gap. As you told me that you have always been faithful to your wife and now all your loyalties lie with her, you should try to convey the same feelings to her, not just in words but in actions too.

The first mistake you made was not coming clean when you began your married life. Winning your spouse's trust is the first and foremost step to a happy and long lasting married life. Now that she feels betrayed, I feel you will have to give her some time to observe you and come to terms with reality. You and your mom will have to be a little patient with Radhika as she is the one who is feeling hurt and cheated. Give her prominence in all family matters. Include her in all your conversations and outings. Remember, she is a part of your family now. As you say, before she came to know about this thing, she was a sweet girl and had adjusted well with you all. I am sure; soon she will understand you fully and forgive you. Time is the biggest healer, Rajat. Her wound is raw right now. Let it heal with time. In the meanwhile, do not show any signs of agitation or impatience,' Meeta concluded.

'I was thinking of taking Radhika to meet Shama, that Muslim girl with whom I was once in love with. She is getting married next month,' Rajat said.

'Has she invited you for the wedding?' Meeta asked him.

Rajat nodded.

'Then this is the best opportunity. Let Radhika meet Shama on her wedding day itself. She will herself realise the futility of her allegations. I am sure once she finds all the pieces of puzzle in place, she will wrap up the whole issue herself. Till then, be patient with her,' Meeta encouraged Rajat who looked quite relaxed by now.

'Hello Rajat.' Rajat got up from the chair as he heard Virender's voice from behind.

'Please sit down. Where are the papers...?'

As the two of them sat discussing their official matters, Meeta went inside to tell Dayaram about lunch and other arrangements.

The evening dawned all too soon for them. Dayaram loaded the luggage in the car's dickey and all of them started towards the airport. They reached airport well in time. As the time came to say bye to each other, their eyes turned misty. Ravi touched Meeta and Virender's feet. When Richa bent down to touch Meeta's feet, Meeta held her on the way, lovingly, 'No more bending down now. Be careful and get regular check-ups done and keep me informed. Eat well.' Then she turned to Ravi, 'Look after my Richa well otherwise I will give you a good spanking.'

Meeta's loving words touched Richa.

Virender looked amused, as he witnessed this loving scene quietly.

'Meeta, your poor son is feeling left out as you have your eyes set on the future target,' he winked at Ravi, who returned his smile with a similar wink.

Meeta looked at Virender, puzzled, unable to comprehend what he was aiming at.

'What do you mean? Who is my future target?' she asked him.

'My would-be grandchild who will inherit your looks and my brains, not like this dimwit of yours who has done exactly the opposite,' Virender joked.

'My son is the most handsome and intelligent person in this world. You better accept it now because I have someone else who vouches for it too. Right, Richa!' Meeta looked at Richa.

Richa smiled and nodded to Meeta.

At that moment, Richa and Ravi's eyes met. The chemistry between them was instant. Richa felt her heart melt when Ravi smiled at her.

Both of them knew that they were heading for better days now.

Their life was going to be milk and roses forever. There would be no thorns pricking their hearts.

They knew their love was there to stay.

They had nothing to fear....neither today....nor tomorrow...never ever.

NOT FOR A LONG....LONG TIME!

Marriage is the most satisfying, most strengthening and most lasting human relationship on this earth

❑❑

Summing up...

We have discussed various problems and situations in this book.

To sum up, marriages are not made in heaven, they come in kits and we have to assemble them.

At first, the joys of romance and marriage make life seem almost perfect. Then, the initial glow of romance fades as the married or committed couple tends to gradually take each other for granted. Partners often become less considerate and perhaps more selfish than they were during courtship. Hence, you must constantly cultivate love in a relationship.

Happy couples show sensitivity to each other's feelings and needs. They act in kind, respectful, tender, patient, forgiving, and loyal ways. They help each other with chores such as cooking, washing dishes, childcare, shopping, etc. These little warm acts add up to a pleasant relationship and keep the marriage strong.

Make it a point to regularly show your appreciation for routine things your spouse does everyday, and for anything else your spouse does that you like. Happy couples show interest in each other's daily lives and share activities. Occasionally do fun things on the spur of the moment. Reminisce together about past good times once in a while.

Keep your relationship alive by being romantic as the years pass. After being together for a while, many couples think they do not the need to express affection to their partners, assuming they well know the strength of their love. Express your love regularly. It is important. Share your feelings so you can receive appropriate emotional support and not based on guesses and intuition.

Happy marriages use honest, open communication about conflicts as the basis for discussion, compromise, and problem-solving, because problems are bound to crop up. Some people try to cope by ignoring them and overlooking their bad feelings, but this solves nothing, rather it builds into explosive anger.

In many relationships, outbursts of anger, yelling, and verbal abuse occasionally occur. Such fighting releases tension and may bring forth important issues that need discussion. This can feel good and may sometimes solve problems, but is an inefficient and often destructive way of communicating.

Every marriage needs a certain amount of humour and acceptance. Don't lose your perspective because of a few frustrating problems. Happily married couples often have recurring, long-lasting issues, but they back off using gentle teasing, appreciation, and affection to break up the tension.

Often a couple's differences actually create a much-needed balance for the relationship as a whole. Man's tendencies towards strong independence balances woman's tendencies towards strong intimacy and makes for a healthy balance.

Forgiveness is particularly important, in reducing tensions, pain, and resentment. Don't rake up the past. A person who regularly brings up the painful past has not been able to forgive and thus strains the relationship.

In happiest marriages, the partners treat each other as equals. Each will consult the other on any important decision affecting both. Sometimes ego comes in the way and mars an otherwise healthy relationship. It is always better to bend a little than to break. After all, marriage is a lifelong commitment.

Many couples feel comfortable with the traditional sex role where the male dominates and the woman submits to his authority. It may work well when the man is considerate, otherwise there are chances of the marriage suffering. Enhance your sex lives by improving sexual communication.

Money is a common source of marital conflict, so try to work together on short-term and long-term financial planning.

Both partners need space to grow. Grow as individuals and blossom as a couple.

Jealousy that interferes with your partner's outside activities or friendships involves negative thinking, and maybe low self-esteem. Replace such thoughts with positive ones. Quit worrying.

Values like honesty, truthfulness, trust, loyalty, mutual respect, faith and a caring attitude are the pillars of a successful marriage. Happiness in married life also depends upon making small sacrifices with readiness and cheerfulness.

Be reliable and responsible. Try to show good judgement and consider the present and future consequences of your actions. Don't abuse alcohol or any other drugs. Live within your means and budget. Stay healthy and fit. Don't criticise in public or make negative comparisons.

Personal problems can weaken a marriage. A bad-tempered spouse can destroy marital harmony while a depressed, sick person may even break it. So look out for the telltale signs.

Marital problems may sprout due to interference and conflicting habits. The families may belong to different religions, have diverse food habits, and attitudes towards life in general. In-laws can also contribute to marital flare-ups. A sensible handling is required in such cases.

Both partners jointly cause and maintain most marital problems, so both will have to change to improve the marriage. Often the blame is laid at each other's door, leading to no solution. Learn to recognise these typical patterns of actions. Develop good communication and problem-solving skills, effective control of anger, and positive thought-habits about your partner and marriage. Remember, polite requests and assertiveness work better.

A little effort on your part to recognise and smoothen out the rough spots will go a long way in making you a happy family.

Enrich your married life and be the envy of your friends, neighbours and people around you!

❑❑

Other Books on PARENTING

125/-

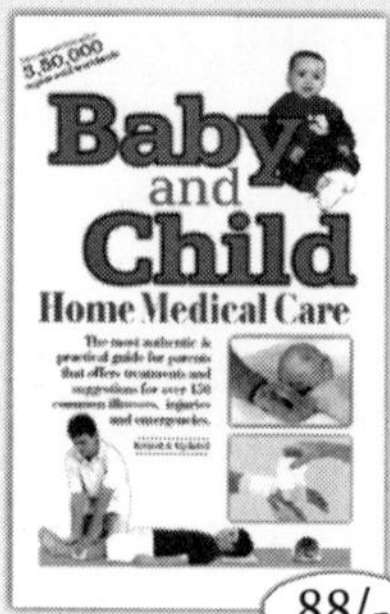

88/-

50/-

88/-

68/-

60/-

80/-

68/-

96/-

Postage: Rs. 15/- each book.
Every subsequent book: Rs. 8/- extra

Practical Parenting Tips

—Vicki Lansky

Over 1,500 Helpful Hints for the First Five Years

Here are just a few of the ideas in this book that parents have actually used to make life with young children easier:

Child proofing:

Keep valuable and small article away from baby's reach. Drape a towel over the top of the bathroom door to keep children from shutting it tightly and locking themselves in.

Tantrums:

Listen. Acknowledge the source of frustration. Whisper in your child's ear. The screaming may stop or turn into a giggle. Disappear into another room. You'll feel better and the tantrum will lose steam.

Hair Care:

Sit your child in a high chair to prevent "wandering." Spread a newspaper underneath.

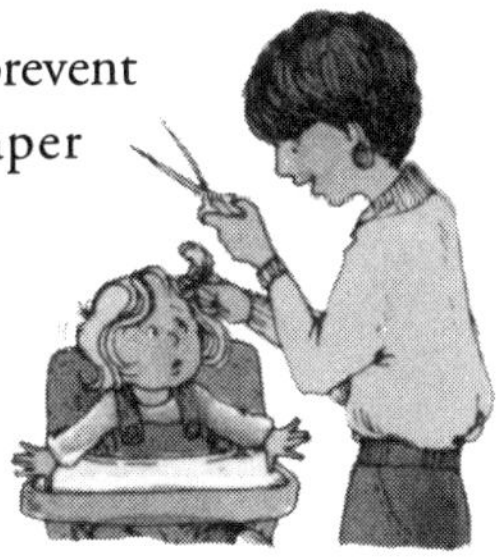

Remove gum from hair with peanut butter. Work it into the hair and then comb out both gum and peanut butter.

Demy Size • Pages: 208
Price: Rs. 80/- • Postage: Rs. 15/-